STORIES
FROM THE
HART

COMPILED BY JUNE WIGGINS

LIMITED EDITION 75 /111

For Nan
with best love

June x

Stories from the Hart

© 2022 June Wiggins

june@thestag.pub

CONTENTS

ABOUT ME

My passion for social history has inspired me for many years. I love researching facts about the past and also meeting so many lovely people along the way. This journey has been extremely challenging due to the pandemic. Lockdown prevented my usual method of collecting stories with face to face meetings and going out and about researching the area. But with video calls and correspondence, I have gathered a wealth of historical records and people's memories, which I hope you will find as fascinating as I do.

I hope the compilation of memories, photographs and memorabilia that I have collected will be enjoyable to all those who read this book. I am a village girl at heart, having been brought up in Kings Langley, Hertfordshire. Now many years later, I find myself living in another village ... Mentmore.

Along with many stories, two significant episodes in this quaint and quiet village of Mentmore occurred in the last century, the sale of Mentmore Towers - the Sale of the Century and the Crime of the Century - the Great Train Robbery. All to be delved into.

My family and I, along with others in the community are now shareholders of The Stag and I am very privileged and excited to be part of all that Mentmore has to offer. Let the stories live on forever!

June Wiggins

INTRODUCTION

Let me tell you a little about the village of Mentmore.

Imagine a balmy summer's day and a journey to the countryside. The roads get narrower and the view is lush and green with the trees and fields and wild flowers blowing in the slight breeze.

It all sounds idyllic and Mentmore really is. You drive up what's known by the locals as "Mentmore Straight" (pictured above).

Continuing on the journey towards Mentmore, the grand mansion known as Mentmore Towers appears on your left (pictured right). A stone's throw away from here is The Stag pub, a welcoming establishment which has served food and drink for over 175 years.

You can imagine being on the set of Midsomer Murders; a well-tended village green, children playing, dog walkers, sheep in the fields, wildlife in abundance and red kites flying graciously in the blue skies above. Mentmore is such a beautiful village; it captures your heart and sparks off memories of days gone by.

For this small tranquil village of Mentmore, it is steeped in history. The community has always pulled together and this continues today.

I am overwhelmed by the input and support of so many people connected to Mentmore.
This book is dedicated to all of you.

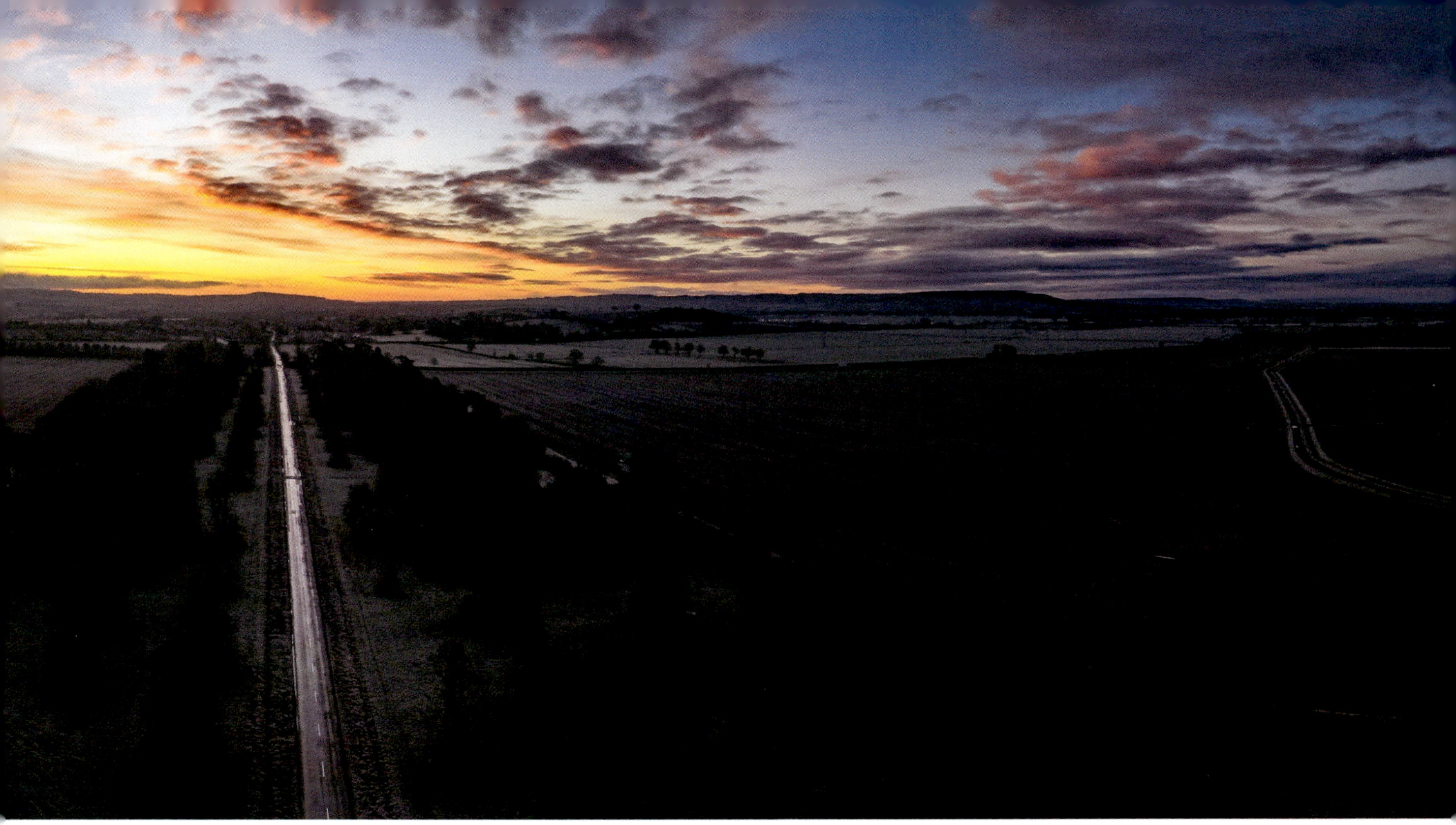

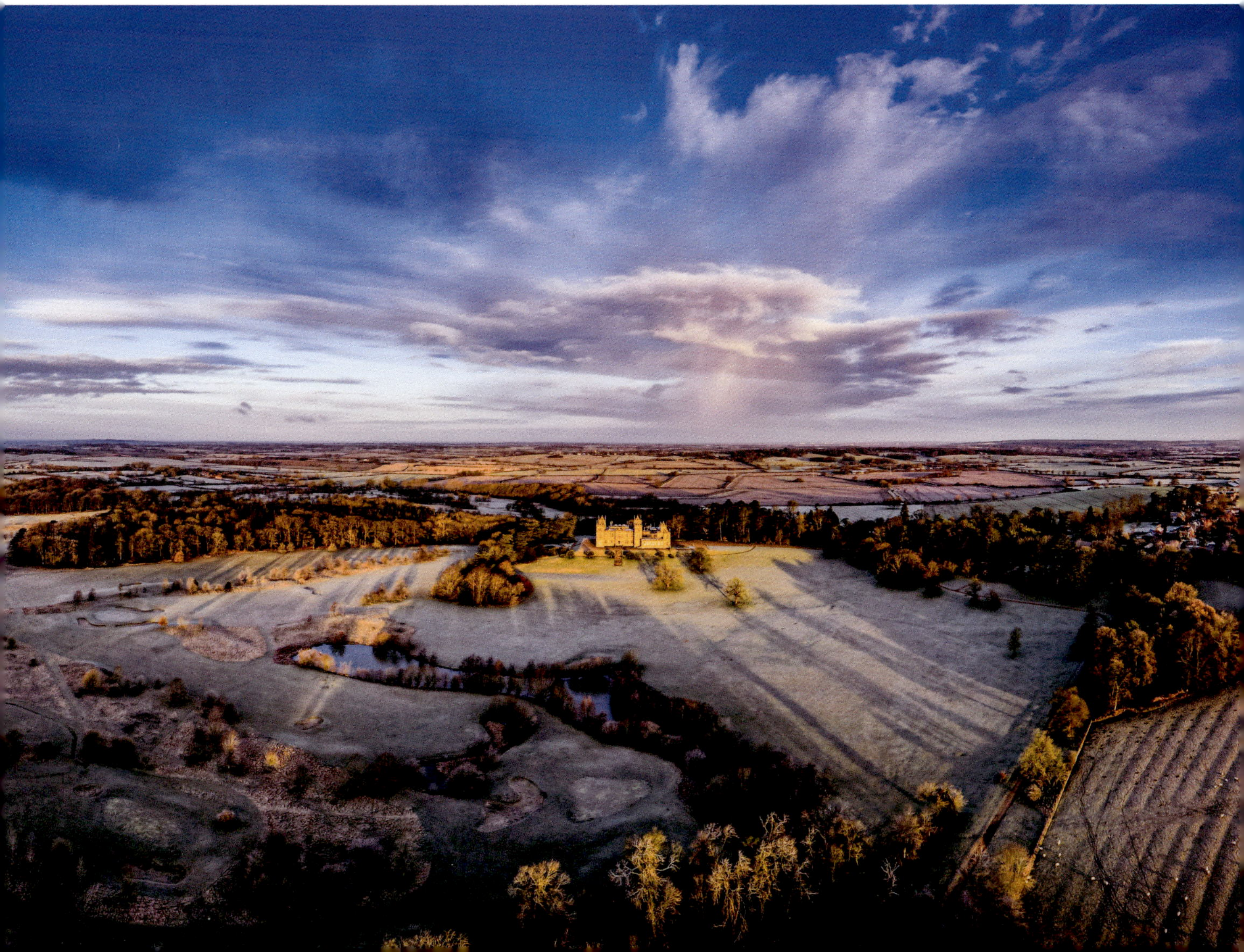

EVOLUTION

The village has changed considerably since the purchase of the villages of Mentmore, Ledburn and Crafton by the Rothschild family in the 1840s; Meyer Amschel de Rothschild was thought to be responsible for having the village demolished and re-sited to make way for his new country house, Mentmore Towers. However, it is documented that the village had remained in situ until May 1877, three years after the Baron's death.

The country house was later known as Mentmore Towers. The Rothschilds and Roseberys were insistent that it should only be known as "Mentmore". Locals called it "The House", "The Mansion" or "The Towers".

Robert Adams, volunteer and guide at Eythrope (Lord Rothschild's private estate attached to Waddesdon) states, "I was once picked up by Lady Rosebery for saying "Towers" and years later by Dorothy Bathurst for the same crime."

The name "Towers" was possibly invented by newspapers and stuck to this day. It's certainly been around a long time, old OS maps just state "Mentmore".

In 1977, Sotheby's who auctioned the estate hedged their bets and used "Towers" once briefly and "Mentmore" thereafter. The catalogues were just titled "Mentmore", as was the SAVE campaign to preserve the house and its contents for the nation.

A plan held at the County Record Office and dated 24th July 1799, shows the estate of Theed Pearse and indicates that the area now occupied by The Stag was just a field with no buildings. This field was part of Warren's Farm, owned by Mr Francis Warren.

Rothschild purchased land at the corner of The Green, the site now occupied by The Stag, together with various lands in Ledburn from the Buckmaster family, a very prosperous family of farmers who lived in Horton in the mid-1800s.

The book "The Wiggs of Mentmore" contains a map dated 1839 which shows a building of identical shape to the present pub building.

The Trade Directory of 1847 lists one Thomas Roffey at "Stag" in Mentmore. By 1851 William Roffey, probably his son, had taken over the running of the pub. In Muson & Craven's Directory of 1853 William Roffey is named as victualler at "Stag" and postmaster in Mentmore.

William was also listed in the 1854 version of Kelly's Directory of Buckinghamshire as being at "The Stag's Head" in Mentmore.

The Rothschild Archive and family now spell Mayer "with an A". The 1977 Mentmore sale catalogue uses "Mayer", but the 1999 catalogue of his silver, spells it "Meyer".

This appears to be the same land detailed in another Record Office document dated 15th December 1810, a Bond of Indemnity (an obligation in writing in which a party has agreed to reimburse the holder of the bond for an injury or loss due to a specific event or has agreed to protect a party from injury or loss related to a specific event) drawn up between farmers Mr John Fountain and Mr Wilkes.

The bond relates to a messuage cottage or tenement, in or near the pightle or backside, a cottage and also

a shop adjoining the cottage at the north end and a barn or lean-to towards the north west side of the garden. That part of the said pightle or backside is on the south side of the messuage cottage or tenement.

As my profession was previously a Registrar, I couldn't resist adding these images of the marriage of Archibald Philip Primrose and Hannah de Rothschild.

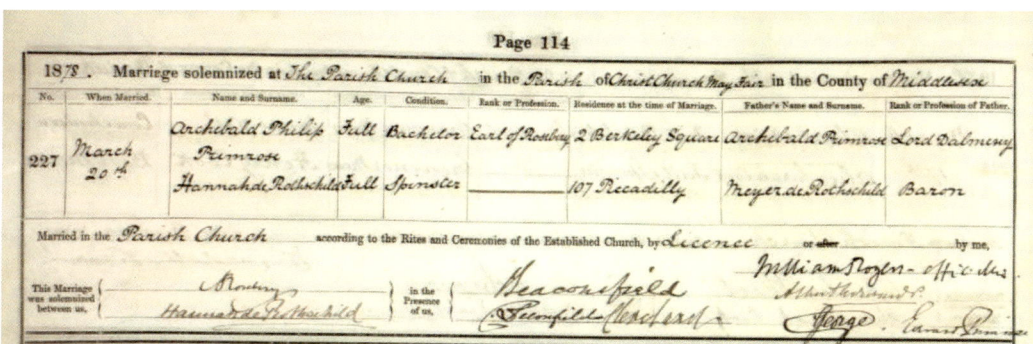

Queen Elizabeth II visited Mentmore in 1964. She came for lunch with Lord and Lady Rosebery and then saw Mentmore Stud afterwards. A very informal business visit as Queen Elizabeth II and Lady Rosebery wore old macs and head squares whilst inspecting the stallions.

The Queen Mother also visited in July 1970.

Mentmore Estate Manager's drawing.

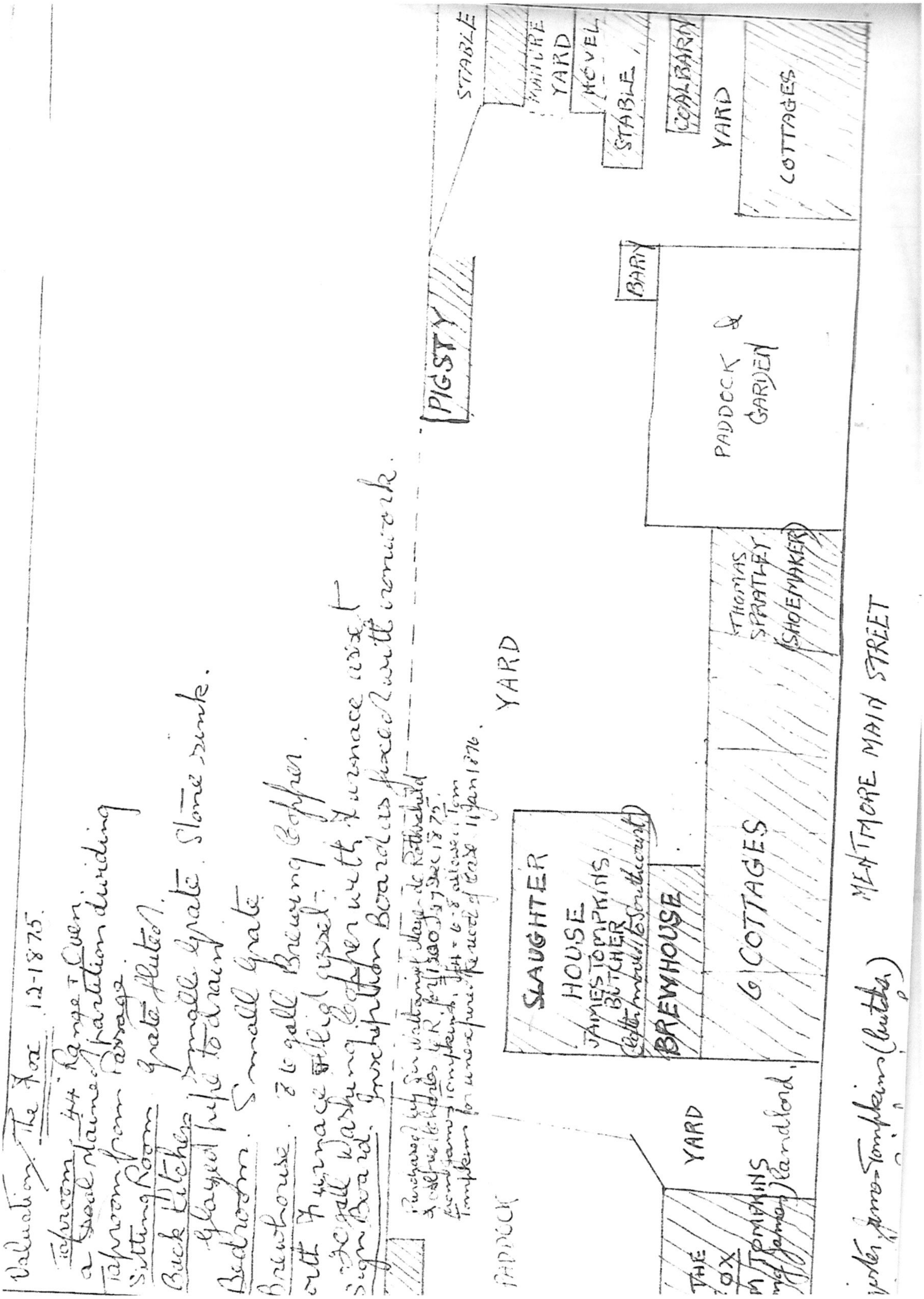

Valuation - The Fox. 12-1875.

Taproom ———
a Good Stained — Partition dividing
Taproom from passage
Sitting Room — grate flutes.
Back Kitchen —
glazed tile to drain · Stone sink.
Bedroom · Small grate
Brewhouse · 3 to gall Brewing Copper.
with Furnace tiling (used).
... gall Washing Copper with Furnace not
... Board ... Furnition Boards fixed with ironwork.

STABLE

MANURE YARD

HOVEL

STABLE

COW BARN

YARD

COTTAGES

PIGSTY

BARN

PADDOCK & GARDEN

YARD

THOMAS SPRATLEY (SHOEMAKER)

SLAUGHTER HOUSE
JAMES TOMPKINS BUTCHER

BREWHOUSE

6 COTTAGES

PADDOCK

YARD

THE FOX
TOMPKINS

MENTMORE MAIN STREET

Information regarding the purchase of The Fox in 1875.

INDENTURE.

Methodist Chapel Mentmore.

Witnessed by James Warner dairyman, John Stevens farmer. all of Mentmore.
" " Robert Sear farmer. William Dickens farmer.   ditto
" " Henry Rogers butcher. Ledburn. Nathaniel Gurney blacksmith
" " Ascott. Joseph Brandom blacksmith Ascott. Christopher
" " Buckmaster labourer of Horton in the parish of Slapton.
" " Joseph Foster wheelwright Stewkley. Rev., Joseph Wilson
" " superintendant preacher of the circuit in the Methodist
" " conextion, agreed to purchase from James Warner for £10
a plot of ground to erect a chapel on the Green in Mentmore. Standing
SW X NE, 40ft by NWXSE 30ft or therabouts, bounded on SW by the public road
and on the East by land belonging to Theed Pearse, all other sides bounded
by land owned by the said James Warner. dated 1832.

Promissory Note.

Trustees of the Methodist Chapel promise to pay Robert Sear on demand
the sum of £20 together with interest . Witnessed this 1st day of December 1843.
William Dickens, Joseph Brandom, Henry Rogers, Nathaniel Gurney.
(This was repeated annualy untill 1850.)

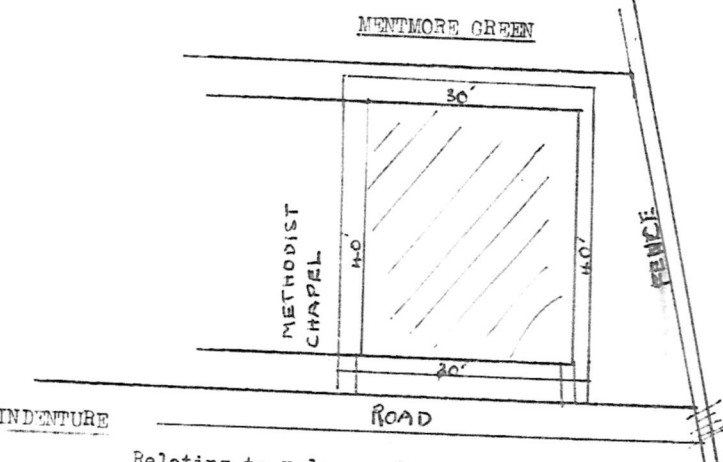

INDENTURE

Relating to release of the Methodist Chapel to Baron Mayer de Rothschild
dated 1851 for the sum of £200.

The Chapel was later made into the village school by Miss Hannah de Rothschild and
at some later date enlarged with the addition of two more classrooms, replicas of
the uniforms worn by the scholars both boys and girls are deposited in Aylesbury
Museum.

The magnificent greenhouses that were situated at the rear of The Stag's garden are now derelict and sadly only the iron work and broken glass is visible. Exotic fruits and vegetables brought back from countries all over the world were grown in these greenhouses.

Cheddington Lodge entrance to Mentmore Towers.

In both the History, Topography and Directory of Buckinghamshire of 1863 and the Bucks, Cambs, Herts Directory of 1865, a Mrs Elizabeth Andrews was shown to be the proprietor of "The Stag's Head" in Mentmore. There is little information available about her immediate successors other than a list of licensees derived from census returns, electoral rolls and various trade directories for the county.

On 18th December 1935, John Nash signed a tenancy agreement with the Ledburn Land Company, which installed him as the new licensee of "The Stag". The agreement gave a full and detailed listing of the contents.

In 1944 during the tenure of John Nash, The Stag was purchased from the Rosebery Estate for £7,500 by the Rt. Hon. Thomas Baron Hesketh.

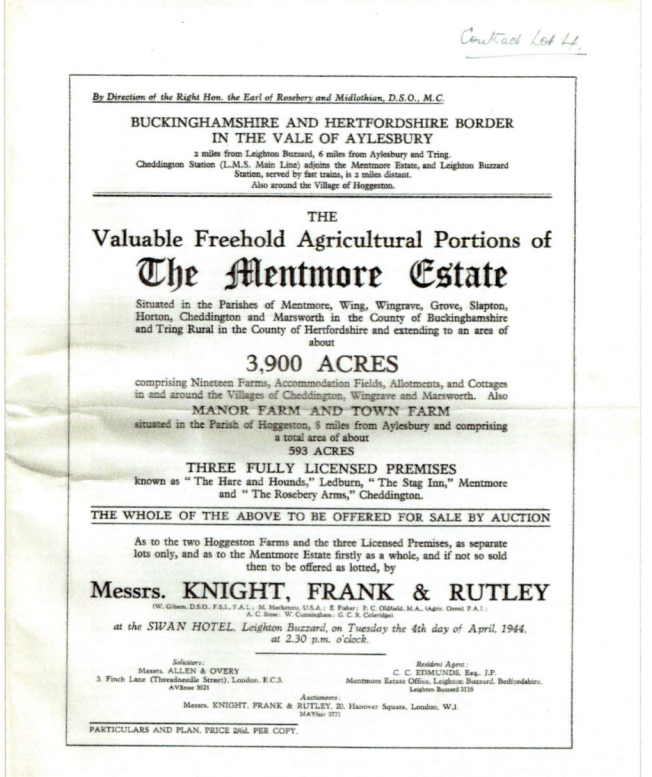

The original sale contract for the The Stag pub in 1944.

As part of the purchase, an agreement was drawn up in July 1944 between the Rosebery estate and the new owner relating to the supply of water to the premises.

Although Hesketh became the registered owner on 17th July 1944, he died three days later leaving his estate in a state of flux. It would seem that although his second son, Frederick, inherited the title and presumably the pub, it was never registered in his name. Frederick died in 1955 leaving his young son as heir. However, The Stag it seems, did not pass to Frederick's son but to his uncle, Major Hon. John Breckinridge Fermor-Hesketh.

A registration appears in the records, dated 13th April 1960, to John Fermor-Hesketh, Company Director.

Fermor-Hesketh died without issue in 1961. In 1963 the Charles Wells Brewery of Bedford, acquired the Abington Brewery Company together with 23 pubs. They retained the pubs but demolished the brewery soon afterwards. However, they did not become the registered owners of The Stag until 13th August 1976, perhaps as a consequence of legal issues following Fermor-Hesketh's death.

It was thought that John Nash was still the licensee when Charles Wells became the owner of The Stag, but certainly within a couple of years, the most well-known licensee of recent years, Michel Rigal, had taken over.

Michel spent over 25 years at The Stag and became an integral part of village life. During his time the old outside toilet block was removed and the rear of the pub was extended to incorporate what is now the restaurant. It was Michel who was responsible for making The Stag well known throughout the Home Counties. While the restaurant had a well-earned reputation for fine dining with an excellent wine list, Michel never forgot the locals. Events included singalongs with Wild Willy Barrett, produce competitions and New Year's Eve parties.

After Michel's departure in the early 1990s, there was a succession of new tenants and a few changes but for the most part, the basic nature of the pub remained - a friendly, relaxed atmosphere in which both locals and visitors could enjoy a quiet drink or meal, in either the bar or restaurant.

Unfortunately, The Stag has undergone several periods of closure in more recent years.

The restaurant was run with an Italian theme as "Il Maschio" by Formula 1 racing driver Mark Webber's partner, Ann Neal, from 2006 to 2013. That business collapsed in May 2013 and The Stag remained closed until November 2014.

This period of inactivity came to an end in November 2014 when Denise Redding and Simon Sparrow took over. They had actually first met at The Stag while both working for Michel, to whom they paid homage by naming the public bar "Froggy's Bar"; French-born Michel was known affectionately as "Froggy" to his local friends.

When their three-year tenancy came to an end they decided to concentrate on their other pub, The Queen's Head in Wing.

The tenure of incoming licensees, Graeme and Gary led to another period of closure in 2018.

No new tenant was found and after prolonged negotiation, in March 2020, Charles Wells Brewery agreed to sell the freehold to a group of local investors, under the name The Stag at Mentmore Ltd.

Plans for a major renovation and refurbishment were drawn up and after a huge amount of work, the pub re-opened its doors on 21st June 2021. Now owned by the community for the community and beyond.

OWNERS OF THE STAG

1844	Land owned by Buckmaster.
1844	Land & buildings at the SW corner of The Green, purchased by Baron Meyer Amschel de Rothschild.
1844 to 1847	Renovation of new build carried out for Baron Rothschild. It is possible that this was done by Stokes because he was responsible for much of the work being done for the estate during this period.
1878	Rothschild to Rosebery by the marriage of Hannah Rothschild to the Earl of Rosebery.
17th July 1944	Rosebery Estate sold The Stag to Rt. Hon. Baron Thomas Hesketh for £7,500. Hesketh set up the Abington Brewery Company in 1942 and The Stag presumably became one of their licensed premises following the purchase from the Rosebery Estate.
13th April 1960	The Hesketh Estate eventually passed to Hon. John Breckinridge Fermor-Hesketh and he became the registered owner in April 1960.
1963	Abington Brewery sold the pub to Charles Wells Brewery.
13th August 1976	Charles Wells Brewery become the registered owners.
March 2020	Charles Wells Brewery sold to Mentmore Community Group: The Stag at Mentmore Ltd.

LICENSEE LIST

Thomas Roffey	1847
William Roffey	1851, 1852, 1853
Jonathan Andrews	1861
Mrs Elizabeth Andrews	1865
Richard Turney	1869, 1871 & 1872
John Mercy	1876 & 1877
George Rowe	1881, 1883, 1887, 1891, 1895 & 1899
George Felce	1901, 1903 & 1907
Ernest William Rowland	1911, 1915 & 1918
Albert Carter	1920
Thomas Hicks	1922, 1924, 1925, 1930 & 1931
Mrs Mildred Hicks	1935
John Nash	Dec 1935, 1939, 1946 & 1951

John (Jack) Nash was probably here until Michel Rigal took over.

Michel Rigal	1964 – 1993
Christian & Carol Wioland	October 1993
Geoff & Maggie Smith	1993? – October 1996
Roger Grey	October 1996
William & Mandy Hay	?? – March 1999
Mike & Jenny Tuckwood	Spring 1999
Ann Neal	Nov 2006 – May 2013
Closed	May 2013 – Nov 2014
Denise Redding & Simon Sparrow	4th Nov 2014 – Nov 2017
Graeme & Gary	Nov 2017 – Oct 2018
The Stag at Mentmore Ltd	March 2020

N.B. The Electoral Register for 1966 notes that Helen Rigal and Thompson & Olga Garbett are living at The Stag in Mentmore. No mention of Michel, so presumably, as a Frenchman, he was not entitled to vote.

Richard Varney was listed as a butcher, beer retailer and farmer. He lived at the far end of The Green at what is now known as "The Old Fox".

The census returns state he lived at the "Beer House", one of the pre-existing dwellings prior to Rothschild's purchases, which was known as The Fox. It would have been owned and run by the occupier, in this case Richard Varney, who brewed and sold beer from his own home. It is possible that for a time he provided the beer for the newly opened Stag. Richard Varney was still named as a beer retailer in Mercer & Crockers 1871 Directory, but not on the Mentmore census. However, in the Harrod's Directory of 1876 Thomas Tompkins was named beer retailer.

The County Record Office pertaining to the policies held by the estate with the Alliance Assurance Company lists the buildings insured as part of The Stag Inn.

> Stag Inn & associated properties (Wash House, Fuel House), Forrester's Office & Club Room (adj. Wash House & Fuel House), Closet adj. Forrester's Office, store and loft over.

> Village club house adj. last above.

The Village Hall was apparently built as two cart sheds, presumably to be used by The Stag and its visitors.

On viewing the Fire Insurance Policy, it seems the Village Hall and associated buildings were originally included as part of The Stag Inn and were insured accordingly. The buildings were separated from the pub at the time of its sale in 1944.

The Village Hall/Club Room was used by the men of the Parish as a club room; it apparently was on two slightly different levels and included a pool/snooker table and a dart board.

The use and running of the Hall was handed over to the Mentmore Women's Institute (W.I.) in 1937. Once the W.I. were disbanded, the Parish Council took over the day to day running of the Hall and it was eventually signed over to the Parish Council in December 1982.

Before the village was connected to the main sewerage system (circa early 1990s) the properties along the south side of The Green, presumably including The Stag, had their sewerage deposited in what was locally known as "the clanger". This was a somewhat archaic system consisting of a large metal tank at the rear of the cottages and which, predictably had its own unique smell and sound as it tipped from side to side as it filled up.

COUNTY OF BUCKINGHAMSHIRE.

T. KYLE,
COUNTY INSPECTOR.

OFFICE OF WEIGHTS, MEASURES & WEIGHING INSTRUMENTS,

COUNTY BUILDINGS,

AYLESBURY, 11th Dec. 1899.

Sir,

A short time since I paid an official surprise visit to the public houses kept by Charles Sayell, Ledburn, and G. Rowe, Mentmore, and I found that they had in their possession for use for trade several unstamped measures for which they are liable to a fine of £5 for each measure as per enclosed notice.

As I am informed that the ... belong to His Lordship, and knowing

that such irregularities would be contrary to his wishes, I have decided to bring the matter under your notice and to ask if you would be so good as to take what steps you consider necessary to prevent the law being broken again.

Yours faithfully,

T. Kyle.

Knight Bruce Esq,

Agent to the

Right Hon: the Earl Rosebery,

Leighton Buzzard.

THE ROAD TO MENTMORE 1819

On the left, as we ascend the hill of Mentmore is Berrysted House, said to have been the seat of Henry of Blois, Bishop of Winchester, brother to King Stephen. It is now a farmhouse belonging to the Earl of Bridgewater. In the Parish Church which is a handsome Gothic building are some memorials of the family of Duncombe who had a seat near here called Barley End House, the property of their representative, Mrs Lucy. On the north side of the Chancel is an ancient altar tomb with effigies of the deceased, said to have been that of the brother of King Stephen, meaning perhaps the above Henry de Blois. Browne-Willis the antiquarian supposes it to be the tomb of Peter Chaceport.

Berrysted House is a place celebrated in the annals of ignorance and credulity for having once been the terror of its inhabitants. Whilst occupied a few years since by a farmer, his different friends visiting him at that time were continually kept upon their "qui vive" [by] the dreadful noises which were confined to a particular room, [and] are said to have caused his guests to alarm the family at midnight. Some very ludicrous circumstances are said to have occurred here to a newly married couple who had gone to Berrysted to pass the honeymoon:- "Ever valued courtesy!" which not only gave the happy couple the best bedroom, but at the same time a spice of its horrors. The bride a brisk widow of about forty, and some ponderosity, happened to be betrothed to a widower, a slender, honest, jovial fellow who cared as little about the how's and when's of this life as any man in the three kingdoms providing he had a plentiful replenishing of his brown jug. This blade had it seems brought his wife by stage-coach to Leighton, from whence he conducted her across the country to Mentmore by field-paths, evening coming on and with it a storm, the lady was subject to the terrible effects of occasionally hobbling, ankle deep through the ploughed fields, and was by the time they reached Berrysted, completely drenched with rain. Tired and exhausted with fatigue, the fair one proposed an early supper, with which her host kindly accommodated her. After a hearty meal, the lady retired, but alas – not to rest. Rest was completely out of the question; mine host and his guest, who had not seen each other for many years, now set in for the evening, when

"Swallow after swallow came and then they swore 'twas summer."

Hospitality, the old British farmer's boast, was here at its height; each draught of the nut-brown increased their hilarity; until the alarm bell warned them of the "witching time of the night;" a parting jug was mutually agreed on, when as they were pledging each other, a most tremendous crash like that of a rolling-stone falling from the top to the bottom of the stairs was heard and ere the terrified topers could have time to jump up, the door flew open and presented to their astonished eyes the weighty bride, sans cap, sans coat, san shoes, sans everything, with the simple exception of her chemise, bruised from head to foot, and the blood copiously flowing, her eyes standing aghast and vociferating "I've seen him! I've seen him! I have seen him!" The terrified fair one fell into the arms of the female servant who by this time had reached the parlour. The scene as might be expected terminated in a hysteric fit; hartshorn, vinegar and the usual remedies after an hours application, at length restored the fair sufferer to her reason, when she anxiously requested to explain what had occasioned her fright. She repeated her former ejaculations emphatically declaring, that she had by the glimmer of the taper's light positively seen – what? - a rat running across the floor!

Now as the farm happened to be plentifully stocked with those quadrupeds, there can be no doubt that these were the terrible phantoms that the disturbed the slumbers of visitors to Berrysted.

Mentmore Village is situated on the crown and around the base of a conical hill, the top of which forms a circular plot of ground has much the appearance of a Roman station; it belongs to the Hundreds of Coteslow, in the Deanery of Mursley and the living is in the gift of Trinity College, Cambridge.

Mentmore Church stands on the left of the road, at the eastern extremity of The Green; the views from hence are very delightful and command the surrounding country in every direction. Wing Park, a pleasant spot, is seen in the north-west direction, with part of the Vale of Aylesbury. On the south-east side of this hill, the whole range of the Chiltern Hills, and in the vale beneath them, the Grand Union Canal is viewed in all its windings.

Written by Dorothy Bathurst, in 1977/8; for Cheddington School children who were being shown around the village. Dorothy was the last Estate Secretary and knew everything there was to know about Mentmore.

THE STAG THROUGH THE AGES (CIRCA DATES)

1892

1901

1935

1968

1986

1998

2001

2022

2020

2015

2013

2012

2010

2007

Police at the scene of the crime in disbelief.

MENTMORE

CRIME OF THE CENTURY

There have been two significant occurrences in our sleepy little village of Mentmore.

The first being the Great Train Robbery on 8th August 1963.

Fifteen men were involved in the robbery, led by Bruce Reynolds, who held up the night train from Glasgow to London.

The gang made off with £2.5 million (the equivalent of £50 million today) which were in 120 sacks.

The robbery was meticulously well thought out to every tiny detail. They had tampered with the signals in the middle of the night and the train was stopped at Bridego Bridge near Mentmore.

They made a human chain and the sacks of money were distributed into their cars which were parked in the lane by the bank of the railway. The haul was carried out within 20 minutes, but because they had a strict time limit, eight sacks out of the 120 were left behind.

Telephone lines were cut in neighbouring farms, but a railway worker who was left on the train saw a passing goods train and managed to call for help.

The gang of robbers were caught by Scotland Yard and were sentenced to 30 years in prison. However, Ronald Biggs escaped and fled to Brazil, where he was caught 40 years later.

Many films, books and TV series have been made about the robbery.

Over the years there have been numerous signs erected on Bridego Bridge, stating this was where the train robbery had taken place.

Unfortunately, these signs have been removed by train enthusiasts wanting a souvenir of this famous piece of history.

The railway bridge is indistinguishable now. The replacement sign above has no mention of the robbery.

To this day the Train Robbers Bridge attracts many visitors who park in the lane and take photos of this famous landmark.

Angela Bowles from Bridge Farm, just up the lane from Bridego Bridge where the Great Train Robbery took place in 1963, has a collection of memorabilia and signed photographs of the Train Robbers' gang.

Although no evidence has been found, there is a whimsical thought mentioned by the locals at The Stag, that the gang could have possibly met at The Stag for a few pints of beer, as they would obviously have met up together to survey the local area before the robbery took place. Indeed, another whimsical thought was that locals at the time were expecting to find money at the scene and searched for many years after the robbery.

... the second major incident in Mentmore, was the "Sale of the Century".

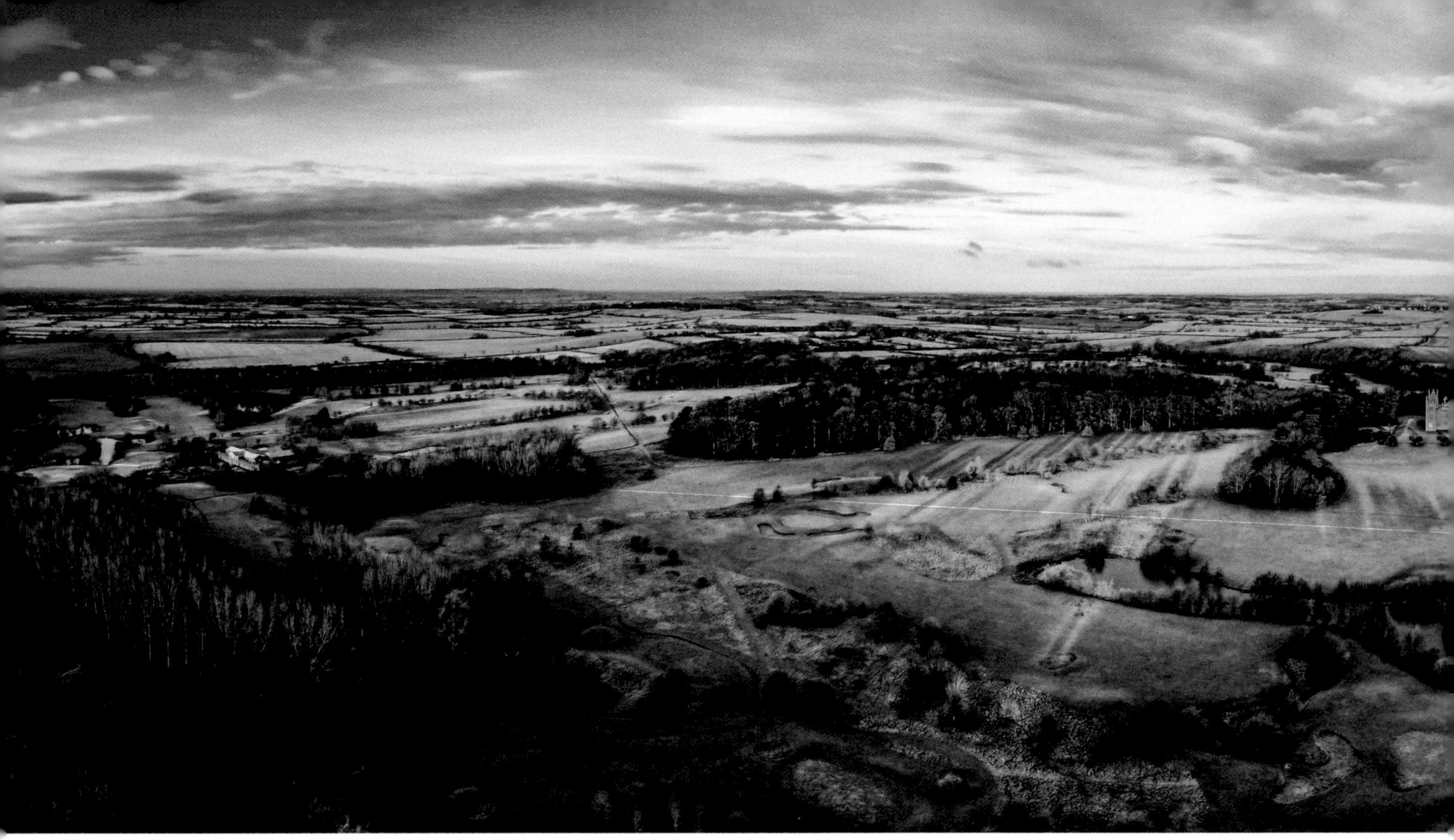

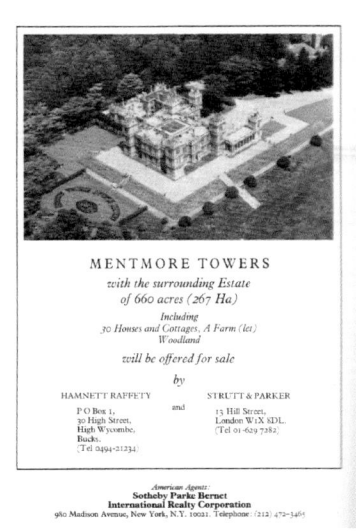

SALE OF THE CENTURY

Mentmore (known now as Mentmore Towers) went up for auction through Raffety's and Sotheby's in 1977 and was labelled "The Sale of the Century". The contents were sold seperately to the property and raised considerably more money. The empty house along with 80 acres of land sold for about £220,000.

MENTMORE
VOLUME FIVE

CATALOGUE OF THE
GENERAL CONTENTS
OF THE HOUSE

Sold on behalf of the Executors of the 6th Earl of Rosebery and his family

which will be auctioned by

SOTHEBY PARKE BERNET & CO.
34 & 35 New Bond Street, London W1A 2AA
Telephone: 01-493 8080 Telex: 24454 SPBLON G

at

MENTMORE, BUCKINGHAMSHIRE
(Telephone during view and sale: 02-96 61515)

PARTS I–IV
in the Mentmore Riding School
on
Saturday, 21st May, 1977 at 11.00 a.m. (Lots 1201–1398)
and at 3.00 p.m. (Lots 1401–1574)
Thursday, 26th May, 1977 at 11.00 a.m. (Lots 2801–2981)
Friday, 27th May, 1977 at 11.00 a.m. (Lots 3201–3375)
AND
PART V
in the Main Marquee
at 3.00 p.m. (Lots 3401–3739)

Admission to the View by catalogue only

(For viewing times see page v)

In sending commissions this catalogue may be referred to as 'MENTMORE'

MENTMORE TOWERS
with the surrounding Estate of 660 acres (267 Ha)
Including
30 Houses and Cottages, A Farm (let)
Woodland

will be offered for sale

by

HAMNETT RAFFETY
P O Box 1,
30 High Street,
High Wycombe,
Bucks.
(Tel 0494-21234)

and

STRUTT & PARKER
13 Hill Street,
London W1X 8DL.
(Tel 01-629 7282)

American Agents:
Sotheby Parke Bernet
International Realty Corporation
980 Madison Avenue, New York, N.Y. 10021. Telephone: (212) 472-3465

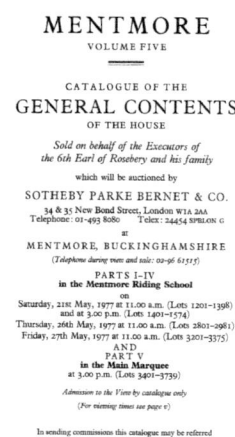

People came from far and wide for this international sale, not only for the buildings and land, but also for the vast amount of antiques inside this grand 19th century country house.

Some of the locals were employed to work at the sale from helping in the catering marquees to handing out sales brochures. This was quite something as people were delighted to get a glimpse inside Mentmore Towers. Catalogues for the sale had been ordered by collectors and dealers in 70 different countries.

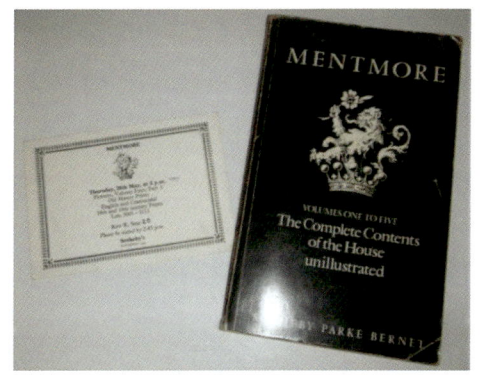

THE GREAT SALE OF 1977
BY ROBERT ADAMS

There are lots of stories and myths around the 1977 sale of Mentmore Towers and the events preceding it, some more fantastical than others, so here are the hard facts and you can judge whether the Government's decision not to acquire the house as a museum was right or wrong.

Following the death of Harry, 6th Earl of Rosebery, his son, the 7th Earl, took the decision to sell Mentmore. Confronted by death duties of £4.5m*, he first offered the house and collection to the nation for between £2,000,000 and £3,000,000. After extensive and protracted negotiations, the Labour Government declined his offer and demanded payment of the death duties in full. A campaign led by eminent art historians, SAVE Mentmore for the Nation, also failed.

Between 18th May and 23rd May 1977, Sotheby's sold the contents of the house and raised £6,389,000. There were too many items sold to mention individually, but here are some details of the most notable and a couple you may not have known were in Mentmore at all. Most of the former collection can now be found in major museums and galleries around the world. This included one of the most comprehensive collections of Renaissance Limoges enamels ever assembled, a collection of 18th century amber plus a collection of 16th and 17th century silver. Also lost to the nation were numerous pieces of furniture by André-Charles Boulle, J-H Riesener and David Roentgen - three of the greatest furniture makers of all time.

In lieu of death duties, the Government accepted a value of £500,000 for the early 18th century Augustus III desk, the 17th century Marie de Medici cabinet and Thomas Gainsborough's only animal picture, Greyhounds Coursing a Fox. Later the National Gallery acquired a Fragonard mistakenly in 1977, attributed to Van Loo - the only bargain.

Several public bodies also spent large sums: The National Gallery purchased two important paintings for just under £1,000,000, the National Gallery of Scotland purchased Moroni's Portrait of a Scholar for £30,000 and the Victoria and Albert Museum acquired a further five items for an undisclosed sum. The total sum of public money spent was over half of Lord Rosebery's asking price for the entire collection. Other private British museums also made numerous purchases.

The public outcry around the Mentmore sale led to a House of Commons Expenditure Committee inquiry, which resulted in the National Heritage Act of 1980 and the founding of the National Heritage Memorial Fund. This is designed to prevent such a cultural loss to the nation from happening again.

The empty house with 80 acres of gardens and grounds was sold a year later for approximately £240,000. When last assessed in 2019, the house was considered by Historic England to be in poor condition with an immediate risk of further rapid deterioration and loss of fabric. By now (2021) this may have changed for the better or the worse.

*Figures quoted by Sir Roy Strong: Splendours and Miseries: The Roy Strong Diaries, 1967-87.

MAHARISHI GROUP BUY MENTMORE

Daily Telegraph Reporter

THE international meditation sect headed by Maharishi Mahesh Yogi the Indian mystic, has paid over £200,000 for Mentmore Towers, the family home of the Earl of Rosebery.

The World Government of the Age of Enlightenment hopes to turn the 100-room Victorian mansion in Aylesbury, Bucks, into a training centre.

The sect plan to send teachers and disciples of the guru to the world's trouble spots as part of its "world peace project." Teams are at present "meditating" in Persia, Rhodesia, South Africa and Bangkok.

A spokesman for the Maharishi International College in Kent said last night: "It is a beautiful place. We love it and will use it for intensive training courses as well as scientific research."

£6·3m art sale

Mentmore Towers came on the market 21 months ago, and last year its art treasures, gathered from all over the world, were sold for a total of £6,300,000.

The 6th Earl died in 1974, aged 92, and duty due on his estate was £9,500,000. At one stage the building, its contents and 600 acres of tenanted farmland were offered to the nation for £3 million, but was turned down by the Government.

The Maharishi, who sprang to fame when he took the Beatles to meditate in India, is now based at is international headquarters in Switzerland.

Although no one is prepared to disclose the exact cost of the transaction, the agents for the executors of the 6th Earl, Hammett Raffety acting with Strutt and Parker, indicated it could be bought for about £250,000.

Mentmore Towers was sold to the Yogi Mahesh Maharishi Transcendental Meditation Movement. It is rumoured that the purchase was funded by none other than George Harrison of The Beatles.

In 1992, Mentmore Golf and Country Club was established, then in 1999 Mentmore Towers was purchased by an investor who is believed to be the current owner (as of 2022).

Over the years Mentmore Towers has been the location for many famous films, Music Videos and TV Series:

1982	Roxy Music: Avalon	1997	Incognito
1985	Brazil	1999	The Mummy
1986	Daryl Hall: Dreamtime	1999	Eyes Wide Shut
19987-2000	Inspector Morse	2000	Quills
1989	Slipstream	2001	The Mummy Returns
1991	Duel of Hearts	2002	Ali G Indahouse
1992	Cherubim & Seraphim	2003	Johnny English
1993	Haddaway: What Is Love	2003	Chaos and Cadavers
		2005	Batman Begins

BUCKS HERALD   www.bucksherald.co.uk   Wednesday, March 16, 2022

Experts visit 'Batman' towers with hope for full restoration

BY JAMES LOWSON
Reporter
james.lowson@jpimedia.co.uk

Officials have inspected a famous luxurious mansion near Leighton Buzzard in the hope of restoring the building to its former glory.

Mentmore Towers, an iconic building which was immortalised in Hollywood favourites Eyes Wide Shut and Batman Begins, now sits derelict.

The moribund state the building is currently in came to the public's attention after popular Instagram account @ Places_forgotten, posted pictures inside the gigantic property.

In response to this, officials from Heritage England and Bucks Council have visited the site to start a potential reclamation project.

Bucks Council and Historic England officials used a police escort to inspect the current state of the building.

A Historic England spokesman said:"We are working closely with the owners and Bucks Council to ensure a positive future for Mentmore Towers and parkland.

"Historic England staff visited the property on Tuesday with heritage and planning officers from the council to review the general condition of the Grade I listed building and Grade II* landscape, both of which are on the Heritage at Risk Register. Our staff were shown around the house and grounds. The police attended to ensure access."

"Mentmore is the first of the grand Rothschild mansions built in Aylesbury Vale. It was designed by Sir Joseph Paxton, best known for designing the Crystal Palace, and was one of the earliest houses to have the home comforts of an inbuilt hot water and central heating system."

Bucks Council confirmed it is working with the body to secure Mentmore Towers' long-term conservation".

Issues maintaining the building are linked back to its sale in 1997 to property tycoon Simon Halabi.

The property developer hoped to turn the famous mansion into a 171-suite, five-star hotel.

A Daily Mail report suggests that Halabi's plans for the mansion were scuppered by the 2008 financial crisis.

Mr Halabi was declared bankrupt in 2010, as a direct result of the plummeting financial markets.

In previous years, a judicial challenge, which the tycoon won in 2007, had previously halted his plans to do business at the mansion.

The photographer who highlighted the decay, Ben James said: "Sadly now most of it is falling apart and needs gutting, which is such a shame."

Christian Bale starred in the 1989 film Batman Begins, which shot some scenes at Mentmore Towers

School's diabetes care wins top award

An Aylesbury school has been recognised with a prestigious award praising its ability to care for pupils with diabetes.

Aylesbury High School (AHS) has been granted the 'good diabetes care in schools' title for the work staff have done supporting children and teenagers with Type 1 diabetes.

"Making sure all of our students' medical needs are met to enable them to thrive at AHS is really rewarding," said Mrs Nix, the school's matron.

"This award is about the whole school community supporting each other and shows the caring community we cherish."

Mr Scobie, headteacher, said:"Well-being and inclusivity are key priorities for our school and we are delighted and honoured to be receive this award in recognition of the work we have done"

"We really value the support of our parents and carers."

Following videos and photos taken by urban explorers, Buckingham County Council, Historic England and the police inspected the current state of Mentmore Towers on 1st March 2022. It was widely publicised and about a week later two tresspassers were arrested.

Mentmore 2010

ST MARY'S CHURCH

The Mentmore community donates funds for the church's upkeep. This includes events such as the Mentmore Arts Festival, which is held yearly over the Whitsun Bank Holiday weekends. In 2012, Mentmore 200 Club was formed.

This article was typed in the 1950s. The tombstone is still there, exactly as described.

The Morning Chronicle
London Friday November 29 1822.

At Mentmore, near Leighton Buzzard, there is a library of books which has no legal claimant. It is a considerable collection of Divinity, Greek and Roman Classics, English History, and has probably been much larger than it is now. It belonged to the Rev. William Beasley, (cannot trace Joseph Beasley) who, about a century ago, was Minister of the Parish of Mentmore, and who, John Horneby says, hanged himself in his study, upon seeing a corpse coming over the green from Leybourne, a hamlet of Mentmore. He lies buried under a plain long narrow stone in the churchyard, at the east end of the church, between the church and the gate. All that seems to be remembered of him besides is, that he paid his addresses to the widow of a wealthy farmer, who lived near the church, and was rejected by her. He appears, from the name occurring in his books, and other circumstances, to have had a sister residing with him, either constantly or occasionally; and a Miss Beasley, probably the same person, married into a neighbouring family. His books are in the care of the Churchwardens of the Parish, and are kept in a small low room of a cottage near the Church, which is said to have been the study where he hanged himself, and the window of which looks over Leybourne-green. From non-usage, spiders, time and dust they are, of course, in bad condition, and afford food enough for melancholy contemplation. - Bucks Chron.

It wasn't easy being a vicar of Mentmore.

The job was within the gift of Lord Rosebery. The 5th Earl liked the sermons to be intellectually challenging, which meant everyone else was lost and the 6th Earl liked them short.

When the pews were moved for restoration in the 1970s, a book on breeding racehorses was found under his pew.

MENTMORE.

A TOUCHING INCIDENT OF LORD ROSEBERY. —A very pretty story is told of Lord Rosebery's home life at Mentmore. It is said his lordship passing the gate of the churchyard met a little girl with a basket of flowers, which she was about to place on her little sister's grave. The great Minister, upon whose judgement rests the destinies of nations, and the little village maiden went hand in hand to the tiny grave, where the fresh flowers were placed. "Do you think your mother would like a stone to mark your sister's grave?" asked Lord Rosebery. The grateful look in the child's face was all the answer needed. Before a day had passed the parents were asked to select an inscription, and in the shortest time possible the stone was placed at the head of the little mound.

As this was such a lovely story, on a very cold winter's day, Irene Webster and I visited the churchyard to see if we could find any more information. Rev. Howard Robson kindly allowed us to view some records in the church, but unfortunately we could not find anything.

Looking into this further, Robert Adams states:

"I looked into the Rosebery tombstone story years ago and came to the conclusion it was a romanticised story with a grain of truth. Mentmore's late 19th century head gardener, James Smith, had several children, mostly girls and a young son who died young. It's quite possible that Lord Rosebery found a sister of Sydney Smith (1877-1886) weeping over her little brother's grave and provided that stone. The carving of Sydney's stone is very fine and remarkably similar to that on Baron and Baroness Mayer de Rothschild's tombstones and also that of Lord Rosebery's wife, all at Willesden Cemetery. Unfortunately, we're unlikely to know for sure.

However, Sydney does have one of the most expensive gravestones in Mentmore's churchyard. It is made of white marble with very finely carved flowers on top. Far more expensive than even a head gardener would probably want to pay for and obviously not by a local mason. It's incongruous when compared to the surrounding indigenous stones in the churchyard.

From the many letters I have, it's obvious that Lord Rosebery respected James Smith very highly, so I concluded that it's quite probable that he paid for the child's tombstone. Smith was very well thought of and appears in many national gardening journals of the time. He and his wife are buried next to their son but have a far less flamboyant tombstone.

The other possibility is that the story is true as originally described, but relates to a child and churchyard near one of the other Rosebery estates."

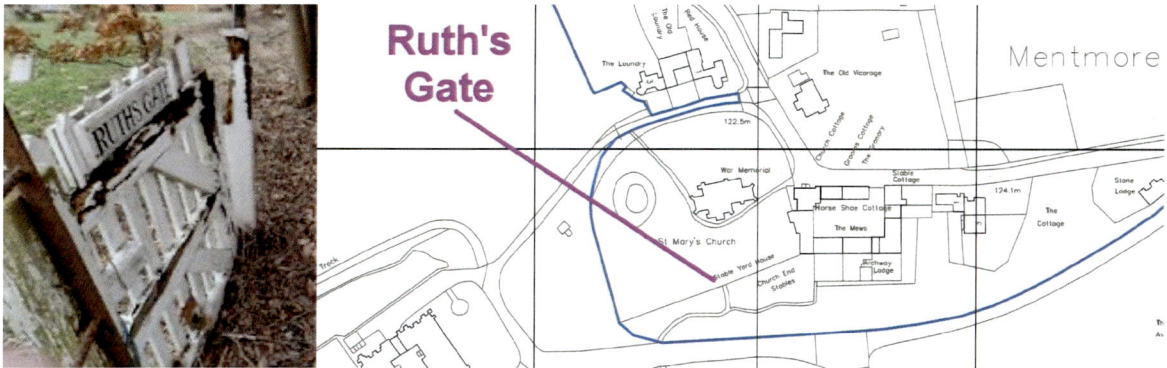

Ruth's Gate in the churchyard is just like any other old dilapidated gate and seems of no consequence at all, but even that has a story!

On the graveyard side the gate sign says "Private", but on the back of the gate you can see the sign says "Ruths Gate".

The whole family used the gate every Sunday to go to church from Mentmore Towers.

At Lord Dalmeny's funeral in 1931, they are reported as using the gate to avoid the press and crowds swarming on the road. In those days a high society event, funeral or wedding, attracted many people.

Robert Adams tells the story about Ruth's Gate, the little wicket gate from the graveyard to the Mansion which was the private entrance to the graveyard of the Earls of Rosebery and their family:

"It has an interesting story: it's named after Ruth Primrose (1916-1989). Ruth was the favourite granddaughter of the 5th Earl of Rosebery. She had a very tragic childhood and consequently spent a lot of time with her grandfather.

Her father was the Hon. Neil Primrose MP, who was the younger son of the 5th Earl, killed in 1917 during World War I. Ruth's mother the former Lady Victoria Stanley married again a couple of years later, becoming Lady Victoria Bullock. Victoria was a fearless horsewoman, so fearless that when out hunting she galloped on a large horse under a low railway bridge killing herself in 1927, leaving the 11 year old Ruth an orphan with only one younger half-sister.

So from that date, Ruth spent even more time with her grandfather. However, Ruth's Gate probably pre-dates 1927 as the 5th Earl never returned to Mentmore after he handed it over in 1922. Two babies from the Primrose family are buried close to the gate, a daughter and a great grandchild of the 6th Earl and Countess of Rosebery.

As a result of being orphaned, Ruth was one of the wealthiest children in England. Her father, shortly before his death, had inherited a fortune from Miss Lucy Cohen, the sister of his grandmother, Baroness Mayer de Rothschild.

Ruth married Charles Wood in 1936. He became the Earl of Halifax in 1959, making her the Countess of Halifax. Like her grandfather and uncle, the 5th and 6th Earls of Rosebery she loved horse racing and was one of the first three women elected to the Jockey Club. The Halifax's horse, Shirley Heights, won the Derby in 1978.

Ruth Halifax died in 1989 and is buried in Kirby Underdale, Yorkshire."

MICHEL "FROGGY" RIGAL

Michel Rigal ran The Stag for nearly 30 years. As well as being an exceptional chef, he was very well respected and loved by the whole community. Born in France, he spent many years in Mentmore and happily accepted his nickname of Froggy, among others.

He is mentioned by many in the following chapter Memories, but I thought it would only be right to dedicate a whole chapter to celebrate his time at The Stag.

Cheers Froggy!

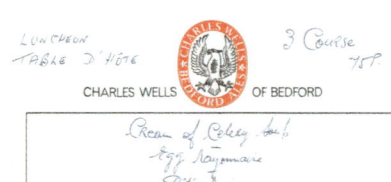

Michel's menu and notes.

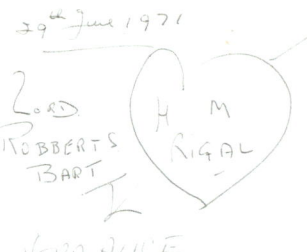

Serving fish off the bone.

Michel and his best
friend in 1974.

Michel's Ford Capri.

Building with the lads (Leo McGurgan and Roger Mildred the Blacksmith).

**RIGAL
Michel
Also known as
'Mr Froggy'**

Passed away on 16th December 2017, in
Stoke Mandeville Hospital.
Born in Paris in 1930 but moved to
Great Britain in 1953 where he spent
the rest of his life. Michel will be fondly
remembered for his time spent as the
Landlord and Proprietor of
The Stag Inn, Mentmore.
The funeral will take place on Monday
22nd January 2018 in the Oak Chapel,
Crownhill Crematorium, Milton Keynes,
MK8 0AH at 12.15pm.
The family have requested no flowers,
but any contributions in memory of
Michel for 'Shelter' can be sent care of:
H.W Mason & Sons
97 Victoria Road, Bletchley, MK2 2PD
Tel: 01908 642700

MEMORIES

A collection of memories from some of the Mentmore people. Several have lived in the village for many years, some have moved away, some even abroad, but their fond and unique memories will never be forgotten and will be preserved forever in this book.

The memories shared are predominantly as they have been written by the individuals. Some stories, however, are similar, but I wanted to illustrate the community spirit within the village.

So get yourself a cuppa and dive right in.

To begin, here are a couple of memories provided by the Mentmore Society Archive ...

A visitor to the pub from Leighton/Linslade told Mike Tuckwood that she remembered when, as a little girl of 5 years old, she would come into the tap room (later the lounge bar) with her parents while they paid their rent to the estate manager.

This was apparently a regular occurrence – it seems he used the tap room, as a convenience for the villagers, as his office was in Ledburn. This could explain rumours that the pub was once the estate manager's house.

The following information was given in October 1997, by Mr Ron Rickard and originated from Albert Rickard.

Sometime during the tenure of Thomas Hicks, but probably in the mid-1920s, the king-stone in the arch of the porch at The Stag was dropping, so the estate builders (Albert Rickard, Len Humphrey and Albert's dad) were brought in to make the necessary repairs.

The stone was acquired from Yirrells and was cut using a stone saw. Before completing the work, they placed a half-crown, a shilling and a sixpence inside an old lemonade bottle and buried it in the porch. Of course, this cannot be confirmed until such time as the porch needs another major rebuild!

Albert & Ron also remember that Tom Hicks' father had an acetylene plant at the pub.

Ron also recalled putting carbide and water in screw-top lemonade bottles and throwing them into "The Moat" (probably one of the ponds in Howe Hill Field) whence they would explode!

Extracts relating to "The Stag" from Thomas W D Hicks's recollections of life in Mentmore, a document in the Mentmore Society Archive. Thomas was the son of Thomas Hicks, licensee at The Stag from the early 1920s to the early 1930s.

I was born in Coventry on 1st January 1915 and moved, with my parents, to The Stag Inn, Mentmore in 1922 when I was 7 years old. My mother's father, William Brazier, was clerk of works on the estate for 45 years. At that time everyone living in and around Mentmore was employed directly, or indirectly, by Lord Rosebery with the exception of my father, the school mistress (Miss Hardwick) and the Parson.

When we first moved to The Stag, we had only oil lamps for lighting. Although the Estate produced its own gas and electricity this was, for the most part, only for the use of the Mansion. Lighting at The Stag changed when my father set up an acetylene plant and provided gas for our lighting. He also provided gas to the village billiard hall, which was next door to The Stag.

Then, when I was about 12 or 13 years old (1927), the large gas holder and the electricity storage plant were taken down and the whole village was connected to the mains electricity supply. The work was carried out by contractors employed by Holland Allfix Cubits; there were nineteen pairs of electricians in the village at the time and many of them stayed at The Stag while they were carrying out the work.

N.B. Some estates, or businesses, installed alternative gas-making apparatus, such as acetylene. The capital costs of acetylene gas plants were considerably cheaper and took up less space and as a result could be located within or close to buildings. Acetylene gas systems made acetylene gas by dripping water on to calcium carbide. The simple process did not require any means of gas purification, however a major drawback with acetylene is its very low flashpoint and ability to explode violently, making gas leaks very problematic.

I remember one particular winter visit by the Prince of Wales; the night before his visit it snowed heavily, and the following morning the snow was so deep that the iron fence and the road from the bottom of Stag Hill to Cooper's Lodge could not be seen.

Lord Rothschild sent out a message stating that every available man was to take a shovel and dig a path for his car, so that it could get from the Mansion to Cheddington Station to collect His Royal Highness. Once the task was completed and the men returned to the village they all came into The Stag for a free beer.

Those who liked a pint were always pleased when they heard that the Prince of Wales was to visit. This was because his chauffeur was usually given money to treat all those who came into the pub to a beer.

All the visiting chauffeurs stayed at The Stag. One of the most memorable visits was when Lord Caernarvon's chauffeur, T Trotman, (he was with Lord Caernarvon at the opening of Tutankhamen's Tomb) came to The Stag – he was stone deaf!

Another "free beer" day was when the local hunt met at the Mansion.

My father kept barrels of beer, bread and cheese in the old fire station building at the rear of the Mansion.

When eggs cost just 1/2d each my mother would pickle several hundred for catering at The Stag. She bottled all kinds of fruit, made pickled onions, pickled cabbage and piccalilli, made her own salad dressing, crab apple jelly and every kind of jam.

ROBERT ADAMS

Under Michel, The Stag was always such a great focal point in the area, I had my 21st birthday there and spent far too much of my youth there! Janet Inglis (Nettie) and her husband, Bob, ran the bar for Michel. They lived at the Old Laundry. Every weekend, there was a great crowd of young people, all of whom were friends. Many of us have aged, many have moved away and, sadly, far too many are no longer with us.

Besides Janet Inglis, another village stalwart was Lily Janes (they are pictured together at a party at Mentmore Stud in July 1984). She was a keen member of Mentmore Women's Institute, a regular church-goer and a long-time resident of the village. Her husband, Frank, I think, had been a gardener at the Towers, but I never knew him. She lived at what is now called Lily Cottage on the village Green.

Over the years I was told many wonderful stories of the village, some of which, I suspect became better as the years went by. When I first came here in the 1970s, we had a marvellous old gardener, Alwyn Kent, who had been born and brought up on the estate; he was full of stories. In their way, the Kent family were as much a dynasty here as the Rothschild's and Rosebery's.

One Alwyn story is that the 5th Earl (the Prime Minister Earl) being an insomniac, would often bang on his Coachman's front door between 2am and 3am and demand to be driven around and around the block between Mentmore, Ledburn. Wingrave, Long Marston, Cheddington and back to Mentmore. He found the movement to be soporific. This story was confirmed to me when I was later told it again by the Coachman's daughter. It's also mentioned in one of the 5th Earl's biographies. The Coachman's cottage was one of the two semi-detached cottages next to the schoolhouse.

Another slightly bizarre story is that sometime after Hannah Rosebery died in 1890, her husband decided the aviary was a waste of money and as he didn't like birds had the inmates killed and stuffed! He then had that iconic aviary photograph taken of the keeper and his family posed with the stuffed birds glued to their perches. Today, many people looking at the photograph don't realise all is not what it seems.

The most memorable story during my time here was in the summer of 1984. Mentmore and the surrounding villages and towns became justifiably terrified of an armed criminal known as 'The Fox'. He was breaking into houses and assaulting the occupants in several very unpleasant and sadistic ways. He was finally caught and given six life sentences for his horrific crimes.

This meant, after several months of terror, the residents could once again sleep soundly in their beds. The police 'Foxhunt' was said to have cost a reputed £200,000, an enormous sum in those days. However, Mentmore had actually been the safest place to be as police had used our house as their HQ because it's a big vantage point. However, we weren't allowed to tell anyone, even neighbours. Consequently, we were the only people who slept well and why the police turned up for refreshments at The Stag every evening! I don't think this is widely known even now.

I'm often asked about the wooden owl, in Ho Hill, the big field along the Ledburn Road. This was placed there after the wind blew a chestnut tree down. It was carved by Les Langley, who grew up at the Old Post Office. It was a random buy at a Mentmore Arts Festival. Sadly, he's getting quite old now and suffered severe injuries during the recent Storm Eunice - I think his days are numbered!

The pamphlet below was written, in the 1970s, by Dorothy Bathurst (1917-2016) for some school children who were being shown around the village. Dorothy was the last Estate Secretary to manage the village for the Rosebery family. An authority on village history, Dorothy bought and converted the former Estate Workshop, overlooking the village Green, into a house for herself, where she lived until the 1980s.

This great house was built for a very rich man, a Jew, named Baron Meyer de Rothschild. It was begun in 1851 and finished in 1857.

But Baron Meyer was not the first man to build here. It is almost certain that there was a Roman camp on this small hill. Roman and Saxon remains were discovered when the house was being built. Several skeletons were found and ancient coins, spear heads, part of a shield and a bronze belt clasp.

We know the Saxons lived here for one of them gave his name to the village. It was called Maenta's Mor which means the land farmed by Maenta.

When Edward the Confessor was King of England from 1042 to 1066, his beautiful wife, fair Edith owned Mentmore and the surrounding countryside, which in those days were forest and moorland. Here they both loved to hunt the stags, wild boar and even wild oxen.

When Edward the Confessor died Duke William of Normandy conquered England in 1066 and became King. During his reign he ordered a list to be made of all his new possessions and written down in the Domesday Book. This book contains information about Mentmore, and in fact the spelling by the Norman clerk is almost the same as today, just one letter has disappeared. He wrote Mentgmore.

THE MAKING OF DOMESDAY BOOK, 1086
William I sent commissioners about the tapestry to ask questions about every existing manor. (Figures reconstructed from the Bayeux Tapestry)

(A copy of the Bayeux Tapestry is in the Victoria and Albert Museum)

Mentmore has always remained a small village with its Church, which is at least 700 years old, the Manor House, Rectory, farms and labourers' cottages. There was one very old farm called Berystede where King Stephen, grandson of William the Conqueror is said to have slept. The farmhouse stood where the cows now graze and was pulled down when the Mansion was built.

It was a love of hunting that brought King Edward and Fair Edith here and 800 years later four brothers, Nathaniel, Lionel, Meyer and Anthony de Rothschild enjoyed the same sport, following hounds all over the Vale of Aylesbury, which was then wild, rough country criss-crossed with streams. They liked this part of England so well that three of the brothers built their homes in the Vale of Aylesbury.

Mentmore was the first great Rothschild house to be built in Buckinghamshire. Baron Meyer chose this position because of the beautiful views in all directions. He asked the architect Joseph Paxton, famous for building the Crystal Palace at the Great Exhibition of 1851, to design a mansion for him to house the art treasures he had begun to collect. His baby daughter Hannah, laid the foundation stone in December 1851.

In 1853 Baron Meyer started a stud farm to breed racehorses. His favourite racehorse was King Tom whose statue used to stand in the main drive and is now in Scotland. He sent from this stud a horse called Favonius to win the Derby. One of the gates into the park is known as Favonius Gate.

The beautiful gates at the main entrance came from Frankfurt Cathedral in Germany. The trees of the main drive were already fully grown when they were planted. They were brought from other parts of the estate and the huge balls of earth attached to them weighed as much as 2 tons.

Baron Meyer was a good landlord and brought prosperity to Mentmore which had been a very dilapidated village. Until he came the fields between Cheddington and Mentmore were a marsh which the villagers had to take off their boots to cross.

The statue of King Tom at Mentmore.

When Baron Meyer died in 1874 and his wife three years later, Hannah became the greatest heiress in the land. In 1878 she married a Scottish Lord, the fifth Earl of Rosebery.

The next twelve years were particularly happy ones for Mentmore. Four children, two boys and two girls were born to the Earl and Countess of Rosebery. Lord Rosebery busied himself with affairs of State whilst Hannah concerned herself with the well-being of the people who worked for them, and feeling it was more healthy for them to live on the hill she moved the entire village from low-lying ground to its present position round the Green.

There was much entertaining at Mentmore and visitors would be taken to see the rare plants in the conservatories, to admire the exotic birds in the Aviary and to lose themselves in the Maze. Many of the trees were planted by famous visitors. Sadly, there is only one tree that has it's plaque naming the King who planted it, all the others have been lost. Hannah's special delight was to stroll with a few friends on a warm summer afternoon through the grounds to the Dairy and there to eat strawberries and cream.

Each summer a Show was held at Mentmore that drew thousands of visitors and cheap railway tickets were issued to Cheddington Station. The chief attraction was a gilded wickerwork car filled with carnations, white pinks and sweetpeas.

In June 1890 Lord Rosebery as Chairman of the London County Council invited all the Council members and their wives to Mentmore. A special train brought them from Euston to Cheddington where horse-drawn carriages waited to bring them to the house.

In November 1890 the people of Mentmore were aghast to hear of the death of Hannah, Countess of Rosebery from typhoid fever. She was only 39 years old.

Lord Rosebery never quite recovered from Hannah's death and although in 1894 he became the youngest Prime Minister since William Pitt he resigned in 1896. For the rest of his life he occupied himself writing books and breeding racehorses. He won the Derby three times. He died in 1929.

The Sixth Earl of Rosebery and his Countess shared a love of hunting. There are many stories of their prowess across country when Lord Rosebery was Master of the Whaddon. They also shared an interest in the Stud and were well-known for their ingenuity in naming their racehorses, as an example 'Camp Fire' was by 'Big Game' out of 'Blue Smoke!

During the last war part of the Mansion was used as a Nursery for small children from London. Later 80 Land Girls were billetted in the house. The Coronation Coach was concealed in one of the garages. It was brought from London on a low loader that used to transport Sir Malcolm Campbell's famous racing car Bluebird. The crown had to be taken off the coach and the roof beams of the garage out before the coach would go in. The Speaker's Coach was also here and many famous paintings from the National Gallery were hidden at Mentmore.

Lord and Lady Rosebery used to spend the months from February to August at Mentmore so that they could follow the progress of their racehorses. True to tradition Lord Rosebery won the Derby, first with Blue Peter, his most famous horse and secondly with Ocean Swell. Both horses are buried near the spot where the statue of King Tom once stood.

When Lord Rosebery died in May 1974 he left his son, the present Earl, with the Scottish estate but there were heavy death duties to be paid on Mentmore, and so in May 1977 there was a Sale at Mentmore of many of the treasures that had been collected by Baron Meyer. Buyers came from all over the world and it was reported in the newspapers and shown on TV as the Sale of the Century.

It is just 100 years since the Roseberys came to Mentmore and so it is appropriate that the Flower Festival in the Church this weekend is a Farewell to the Roseberys.

The great house now stands empty, waiting to see what the next 100 years may bring.

BOB AGER

So many great memories, but to be honest there are so many events that they all blur into one great experience.

I am sure you have already heard about our regular Sunday lock-in spoof games, that went on from 2.00pm closing until evening opening time. Curtains drawn, on one occasion the police called on the pub on another matter, went to the dining area to talk to Michel and although they must have known what was happening decided to ignore the presence of a dozen illicit drinkers next door.

The Pink Nipple Cup! A clay pigeon trophy donated by Deborah Hale-Hall. Lots of somewhat inebriated lunches.

Wild Willey Barratt is another character who deserves a mention.

High Cockalorum contests with associated soda fountain fights.

Lots of expensive champagne when Mark Webber won the British Grand Prix.

Just some random thoughts.

JENNY ALLEN

While Jenny's parents were enjoying a drink in the pub, she remembers sitting in the car outside with a bottle of Vimto and a bag of crisps with the little blue wrapper with salt in.

Frank lived in Mentmore all his life, when he passed away his wife was allowed to live in the "tied" house for the rest of her life.

On the right is her account of her family in Mentmore.

The Mentmore Connection.

In recent years television drama's such as "Upstairs and Downstairs" and "Downton Abbey" have entertained and educated many millions with experiences of life in large country houses, and the involvement of the staff involved in the running of them in the 19th century and up to the time of the First World War, and briefly beyond.

The Janes Family had many members who were employed on the Rothchild / Lord Rosebery Estate at Mentmore, early in the 20th Century. George and Rebekah, both born in 1865 lived in a cottage down the hill at Rowden Farm in Ledburn, where George worked on the farm, tending to the cows and horses. So it seemed logical that a local source of employment for some of their boys was Mentmore Towers.

5 boys.

Frank, was employed as a gardener on the estate. His second wife, Lily who succeeded him was the last sitting tenant of the houses tied to the estate. She died n 2005. By then most of the other surrounding houses had been bought up by wealthy people from outside of the area, often as second homes.

Ernie, Worked with the horses in the stables.

Harry, Married Doris, worked for British Rail in the Transport Police. They eventually lived in Preston Lancs. After their deaths their ashes were scattered on his parents grave, located in Mentmore church graveyard.

Sid, Married to Beatrice Amelia (known as Janet).they lived at 2, Queens,Road in Berkhamsted. He also worked for British Rail. Working night shift shunting at Euston Station, London. When the opportunity presented its self he transferred to operate the signal boxes in Berkhamsted and Northchurch.

Fred, His outcome is unknown.

George and Rebekah Also had 2 Girls.

Mable She married Alf Hirons and he also worked in the stables with the Rothchild horses. They lived in Wing

Violet Marred Clem, he was a London Bus driver, They lived in Muswell Hill, London.

During the 1950's Sid's Daughter Esm'e and her husband Arthur Poll, accompanied by their 2 children, Robert and Jenny, would often travel on a Saturday or Sunday night from their home in Berkhamsted to spend many a happy hour with the Janes Family members in their local pubs. These would alternate between the Stag at Mentmore and the Hare and Hounds at Ledburn. This would occasionally include the White Swan at Cheddington.

Jennifer Allen (nee Poll). 2021

DIANE AND MIKE ARMSON

Firstly Roger Mildred. He was the local blacksmith and worked with his brother, Tony, at 'The Forge'. This stood between the Manor House and the Bothy, it was recently pulled down to make way for new building. Roger was a very prominent local personality, he was very well known and spent much time in The Stag. The Thursday Club was a weekly gathering of local "entrepreneurs" who met at The Stag on every Thursday evening.

These gatherings were obviously heavily alcoholic.

I never joined as my business required me to be able to rise and shine on a Friday morning.

I don't know if you have been told about the times when Wild Willy Barrett, who had quite a famous No. 1 hit with his partner John Otway. He frequently used to come to the pub and 'perform' on the piano. There were some pretty amazing evenings back then.

The 'Thursday Club' and the unusual Sunday drinking hours when payment for the rounds was determined by the results of games of spoof.

MIKE BUCKLE

Inspector Morse was filmed at Mentmore Towers, titled "Cherubim and Seraphim". I spoke to the location man at The Stag and he gave me an Inspector Morse crew bomber jacket.

It was 1991, we did an auction at Cheddington School, I chatted with the location manager about the filming etc. at The Stag. He gave me the jacket for the auction and I bid for it. I think it was about £30. I was the chairman of the PTA and we raised about £2,000.

MALCOLM CLELAND (MAC)

I was a Staggerer. We came here in 2001 when Mike and Jenny Tuckwood were running The Stag. We got the feeling that Jenny was vetting us for the first couple of sessions but we made friends well before she started to do intros. We did get on her good side in the end and would get a tug to dine with them and a group of regulars and friends.

Mike used to be a cook in the Army and produced in his words 'Haute cuisine, Army portions'. Most Mentmorians would remember them. Jenny was pleasant enough but gave the impression that we were being monitored for our behaviour in her 'restaurant'. They threw a leaving party when they left which was more than boisterous and cheerful.

Then we have the racing driver and his wife Ann. She was a sleeping partner with the family that ran the pub, an Italian family based in Leighton Buzzard. I am pretty hazy on the chronology of who and when. I put that down to fumes I might have inhaled there.

Lloyd, who has now passed away unfortunately, used to tell stories about moving the piano from the public bar to the lounge by way of over the bar taps. He said he was nearly sick with laughing at that adventure.

CAROL AND TERRY COX

Terry and I and our daughter Michelle moved to Mentmore in 1987.

Despite spending considerable time unsuccessfully searching for the right home we noticed the advert for our home here in Mentmore in the local newspaper. It did not meet the criteria of reducing travel time for Terry's work, but all three of us felt Mentmore, where Terry and I had done all our courting, was the right place for us.

The Stag was everything in our pre-marriage days and up to when we went to Saudi Arabia. When we got engaged Michel and Helen Rigal gave us a wonderful meal and champagne. We still have the empty bottle signed by them both.

When I became pregnant Michel Rigal decided I was far too thin, so every time we came for a drink he would feed me, everyone will know how lucky that was! He always said - you cannot stay down here with all this cigarette smoke even though he smoked Gauloises at the time! One time Michel, still talking about how thin I was, came over with a pint of Guinness and Port. Well I did not drink when pregnant, so Terry couldn't wait to drink that!

Needless to say I gave birth to a very healthy 8lb baby girl. Terry was very proud and insisted that we took her to The Stag straight from the maternity hospital.

In the summer of 1970 Michel Rigal did a buffet in Mentmore Village Hall. It was his christening gift to us and the spread was amazing.

Eighteen years later Michel and The Stag was the chosen venue for the black tie dinner to celebrate our daughters 18th birthday.

I always smile when I see the black and white photo of Michel and Helen cuddling our daughter outside The Stag, then the photograph of him presenting Michelle with a bouquet of flowers at her birthday celebrations 18 years later. Leo took photographs of the event at the house and The Stag.

We have met and become good friends with so many people in The Stag over the many years we have been drinking there and it has played such an important part in our social life with so many wonderful memories.

Sadly Terry passed away on 4th April 2021.

He did not get to see his beloved pub open once again. However, I arranged for all his friends and family to be there at The Stag to celebrate Terry's life. Everyone enjoyed the celebration of Terry's life, on the day which would have been his birthday.

LIZ AND NIGEL DACK

My parents used to come to The Stag in the 1950s/1960s (from Tring) every year to celebrate my father's birthday, about the only time they went out together in the evening (we used to play the babysitter up meanwhile).

My father brought me to The Stag to celebrate my graduation in 1972. My boyfriend in my early twenties used to bring me there occasionally, so we were slightly familiar with the village. Later when we lived in Hemel Hempstead and saw a poster at Hemel Hempstead station advertising houses for sale in Mentmore by Dutch auction and we bought our house in 1975. You could have a slap-up meal in The Stag for £5 then!

My parents had friends who said they had lodged in The Stag in their early married life (which must have been late 1940s). As far as I know, they had nothing to do with the pub/restaurant trade, just a young couple starting out.

Nigel remembers accompanying his father who worked for Foster Brothers (men's outfitters). His father used to visit pubs to measure the farmers up for suits and The Stag was one of the venues!

Nigel proposed to me in The Stag in 1996, on his knees with a rose clenched in his teeth. I was mortified and said "no" because he was drunk! I gave in later!

Roger Mildred, the village blacksmith, featured largely, as you will be aware. I remember being shocked one evening when he dragged a bale of straw into the bar and announced that his missus was calving. His celebration of the birth of a son!

I worked as a barmaid for a while in the days of Michel. It was great fun. Caroline Gates and I used to run the bar on Mondays when the restaurant was shut. The Stag under Michel was a huge draw, attracting parties of people out from London at weekends. I remember working in the bar over Bank Holidays and there would literally be no room to move.

Children were freer in those days and they all used to spend a lot of the time out on The Green and in the grounds of the Towers, and on their bikes. I used to have to ensure the children were at home in the early afternoon, when all the expense account lunchers would roll out to their cars and shoot along The Green - before the days of drink driving laws.

Also of course when opening hours were more restricted. My son Jason, as a young child (unbeknownst to me at the time) would sometimes go into The Stag, sit down and order a drink as he had seen adults do.

Michel treated him courteously and served lemonade!

He would serve a stirrup cup to the hunters on their horses which was always quite a spectacle.

I used to do a bit of bookkeeping for Michel. If people didn't pay what they owed, he never pursued them! He had Spanish waiters who lived in and we used to suspect they would help themselves to drinks and cigarettes - there was no security. Everyone of course smoked in that era, so an evening in the bar meant coming home smelling of cigarette smoke and cooking.

As Mentmore had been an estate village and all owned by the Roseberys, boundaries were a bit blurred sometimes. The Village Hall was gifted to the village, along with The Green and there were a couple of outbuildings attached to the hall which didn't seem to belong to anyone. The Parish Council at the time let The Stag take one of the buildings over, which they used as a store.

Once an upper room in The Stag caught fire and my son Jason saw the smoke, along with Lesley Langley. The alarm was raised and no huge damage done, and Michel treated my family and the Langley family to a day in London at the pantomime as a reward to the boys. Children from the village decided that they would like some play equipment on The Green. They wrote a letter to the Parish Council requesting this. And once The Stag was broken into - I don't remember the details, but the police deduced that they had waited in our garden until the coast was clear. We got security lighting after that!

The Village Hall was given to the village along with The Green by the Roseberys.

It was the old Women's Institute Hall and used to be smaller at one time as in the Main Hall it has suspended floorboards and the rest is solid.

When I came in the mid-seventies, I don't remember the Village Hall being used except for whist drives and I think beetle drives. They weren't WI meetings, as I remember at least one man being involved, Colin Higgs who came from Aston Abbotts.

There may have been WI meetings as well, but as the estate had more or less broken up by then, they probably wouldn't have been well-attended.

I remember four ladies around at the time who may have been members - Lily Janes, Gladys Ross, Mrs Lindores and the old nanny, Jo. I don't recall her surname.

Gladys had been the teacher at the school, Mrs Lindores was the widow of the head gardener, and Lily had been a maidservant I think. There was also George Pennell's wife and his mother, but I never met them, they didn't really go out much.

In the early 1980s, the Village Hall had grants to refurbish it.

Jennifer Langley and I planted the beech hedge that marks the boundary between the Village Hall garden and No. 35 and we couldn't get it straight along the boundary without a very wobbly line, so we had to leave the apple trees that belong to the Village Hall on the 'wrong' side of the line - they are probably now included in the property of No. 35!

The drains used to be a problem before the advent of mains drainage and we often used to have to unblock them in the middle of functions, such as the Barn Dance on The Green.

You will have heard about the Victorian mechanism (the Clanger) for dealing with waste water before it flowed down into the fields. It was situated below the wall where the greenhouses are and made a loud clanging noise as it emptied its load - which was quite frequent in the mornings when people were having baths.

It had to be emptied periodically and was a sight to behold! The exact location of all the drains is still a mystery and used to be a nightmare when they (frequently) blocked as it was not always possible to know whose responsibility the blockage was.

I think I have mentioned the outbuildings in the Village Hall which were very dilapidated and not used - one was given over The Stag to use. There was a small rowan tree in the middle of the garden which may have been planted in memory of a little lad, son of Mrs Lindores who was killed in an accident with farm machinery. His grave is in the churchyard. The tree was in the way when we started to use the garden for functions and was cut down a few years ago with the idea that the wood would be used - Peter Brazier made some wooden clocks and there is a plaque in the Village Hall.

In the Village Hall in the seventies/eighties we used to have a Christmas party for all the children in Mentmore, Ledburn and Crafton - quite a few at one time. We also held New Year's Eve parties, though not every year as they were often at The Stag.

Later, Jonathan Langley's father David, was employed to do repairs and he was meticulous to a very high degree. Jonathan now looks after the Village Hall with a proprietary interest, continuing his father's work.

Before the original refurbishments, we did a great deal of fundraising - the reason for the annual Barn Dance, and there has been a great deal of fundraising since then which with grants, has enabled the Village Hall to be updated and made into a lovely venue for parties, classes, meetings etc.

I remembered the time when the criminal dubbed the 'Fox' was around and was terrorising the area.

In Mentmore the police were on nightly stake-outs - they were all desperate to be the hero that caught the beast - they would knock on the door at night if a light went on to make sure everything was ok. They would come into The Stag in the early evening and Michel would give them food to sustain them through the hours ahead.

It was a very scary time and from then, everyone stepped up their security and took care to lock their doors and shut windows when they went out. Before that, people didn't bother to lock their doors.

I remember there was a fancy dress party at The Stag. When I took the babysitter home to Cheddington, I was stopped by the police and invited to give them a twirl in my fancy dress! I don't think I was the only one!

I also remember when we had a very bad winter in the 1980s and the snow was very deep. The Stag was fully booked that evening, but none of the people could get to the restaurant as the weather was treacherous. Michel went out and knocked on all the doors in the Village and invited the community to have a meal at The Stag, as the food would have been wasted. This evening was always fondly known as the "Snowstorm Dinner".

It appears that everyone who was a regular at The Stag had their own spot to sit and were most put out if someone else was sitting there.

Mrs Win Denchfield would be carted up to Mentmore by her son and his wife on a Friday night to play the piano in the public bar. Not necessarily a concert pianist standard, but I remember how enthusiastic she was. She loved a good old sing-song.

PHILIP DELAFIELD

My parents knew Michel and Helen and I worked as a student stocking bar shelves when Michel ran The Stag back in the early 1970s.

LINDA DRAPER

We live on Church Street, Leighton Buzzard in a house/land that dates back to the 1820s.

Apparently, there was a cellar in the original cottages and when they were completely refurbished in the 1970s (I think) then crockery from The Stag was dumped in the cellar.

We were told this by the previous owners but as the cellar is now completely sealed now there is no way of knowing.

It's my understanding that there was some relationship between the people living in our house and the owners at The Stag.

DARREL FOSTER KIRSOP

Firstly, I think Michel should be given huge credit for retaining the 'local' nature of the public bar at the front. He realised right from the start that The Stag was the only 'pub' in the village, and that by gentrifying the whole place as merely an upmarket restaurant, he risked marginalising the local types who had drunk there for several generations.

Thus, he retained the slightly 'spit and sawdust' ambience of the public bar, and in the process made himself popular with the mere mortals like myself who frequented it. At the same time, this gave the restaurant side a certain authenticity as a country pub, which the great and the good restaurant users often embraced.

This was reflected in the vast collection of model frogs (well he was French!) that Michel amassed, each being a gift from clients of both the restaurant and public bar. One such occasion I recall supports the above theory.

Sometime in the early/mid '80s, I bumped into Rod Stewart (in the toilets of all places) there, who was making a video promo at Mentmore Towers. I suggested to Rod (who was very down to earth) that after his meal, he might enjoy an after dinner drink and the atmosphere in the public bar. He did just that, and chatted with the locals for some considerable time. Sadly, Terence Donovan, who was directing the video, seemed to think this a bit below his station and stayed grumpily in the restaurant.

In connection with many films and videos that featured Mentmore Towers as a location, I will claim some small personal credit.

When the mansion was purchased by (with George Harrison's money) and became the headquarters for the Maharishi Foundation, in 1978, I had some publicity business with the Foundation, and suggested to their marketing chief that he should list the building and grounds as a location in film industry guides - something he hadn't considered before, or was even aware of as an opportunity - which it proved to be.

Many TV programmes, videos & films subsequently took up this option.

Oddly, this doesn't include Rod Stewart's promo video, nor that of one later made there by U2. The point is though, that many of the stars that visited Mentmore for this purpose will have undoubtedly visited The Stag at close of play.

Finally, I couldn't tell tales about The Stag without mentioning dear old Roger Mildred. With his "Smithy" just across the road, Roger was almost part of the furniture there, but it was after closing time that he really came into his own.

Locals may recall that, in addition to being an excellent blacksmith, Roger was also a dab hand at making country wines. I recall many a terrible hangover after foolishly taking up an offer that typically went .. "Dear boy, you must accompany me across the road to try my new lemon* wine - your expert opinion is greatly desired!"

Of all the characters that frequented The Stag over the years, Roger must surely be among the most memorable.

One thing I didn't mention is that he made several TV appearances (things like Blue Peter) over the years, where the production needed to feature a blacksmith that looked the part - which with his muscular frame and rooks nest of a beard he certainly did.

CAROLINE AND MARTIN GATES

When we got married, Bob Inglis who lived at Laundry Cottages on the corner leant us his Cortina car to go on our honeymoon. The car broke down and we had to spend a lot of money to get it fixed, so only had enough money for a bacon sandwich!

We moved from Ledburn to The Old School in 1981.

Old School House, Mentmore as it was in 1908

Previously Mrs Gladys Ross, a lovely lady, was the school mistrees and was married to the butler at Mentmore Towers. At that time the school had 13 children attending, all of mixed ages, and came from Mentmore, Crafton, Ledburn and Rowsham. Mr & Mrs Ross moved to a house in The Stable Yard and latterly near The Fox pub.

When we first moved into The Old School the building was derelict with no running water, toilet facilities or electricity. We would use a hosepipe in an old sink for washing and went to friends and families for a proper wash.

Mentmore school children in 1928.

The garage was built by Martin and Eric Mitchell.

Next to The Old School was the Chapel and next to that was the School House where Danny Killick, a famous potter lived.

Interior of the Old School in 1981.

Martin Gates and Eric Mitchell.

ROBERT GATES

I played in the fields and woods at the back of The Stag garden. A child's paradise to explore.

The greenhouses, the ruins of which can still be seen, was where exotic fruits such as pineapples and bananas were grown for Hannah de Rothschild.

There was also a sewerage pipe that ran by these greenhouses which over flowed sometimes - no health and safety for inquisitive kids then.

When I was about three years old, there was a fire at The Stag with smoke coming out of an upstairs window. My mum was working at The Stag at the time. The fireman gave me a lift home in the fire engine.

I remember peacocks roaming around on the village Green and seeing the white doves that had been painted all different colours by a gentleman who was a wildlife enthusiast from Crafton...... an amazing rainbow of colours flying in the sky!

This gentleman was an animal and bird lover, he even had cheetahs and monkeys, until there was a petition set up by the villagers, as they were worried the animals could escape.

When I was at Wingrave Primary School we were given a tour round Ivinghoe, Pitstone and Mentmore.

We stopped at the Water Mill and I was recognised out of all the children there as Martin Gates' son. The same happened when we got to the Pitstone Windmill and I was the one to help make the flour. When all the children arrived at Mentmore they stopped off at the blacksmiths. Once again, I was recognised as Martin Gates' son and was the only child allowed to make anything with the steel and hot fire.... I made a golf club!

As I grew up I worked with Roger Mildred, the blacksmith, on a number of occasions. He made all the railings around Mentmore and I had the job of painting them.

There was a strong tug of war team in Mentmore and we won every time, competing all over the country.

Mentmore Village School had to close because there were less than 21 students attending. Sadly the building became derelict for quite a while before my parents moved there in 1980.

I remember the story of the well behaved children at the time who would warm the outside toilet seat for the headmaster. On a Friday, a naughty child would have to clear the toilet and put it all in a wheelbarrow and take the smelly contents to The Stable Yard, which is now named Howell Hill Close. The historic name (as used by the estate workers) for Robert Adams' big field opposite has always been "Ho Hill". He found that it was probably a corruption of "Howell" or "Hugel" which is Old English for a small hill. A map of the farmers of each field showed Mr Howell a local farmer on it in pencil.

Leo McGurgan was a stable hand at the stable yard and he would come to The Stag every day.Even when he left the stable yard, he still came every day on his moped. He was a really lovely bloke.

Of course, many of the people had their nicknames and here are a few:

Twin Tub was Brad Field who was the local Policeman.
Smelly was Alec Davis who was a cattle farmer and then a fishmonger.
Cracker was Nigel Dack, as in Crackerjack.
Brush was Geoff Saville who was a painter and decorator.

Ivor (nicknamed for his love of trains) was one of the regulars and was late going home from the pub one Sunday lunch time. His wife brought his roast dinner to the pub and slammed it on the table in front of everyone.

When Rodney Johnson moved to the village near the Vicarage, he invited all the locals to come for drinks and to bring paint and a paint brush. The room ended up full of graffiti for years and stayed like that until he moved away.

The Dairy (above right), became derelict for over 20 years after the Johnsons left. They sold fruit and vegetables and I remember my mum asking me to walk there when I was young to get provisions.

I have travelled all over the world and whenever I say I live in Mentmore, people always remember The Stag there.

Christmas card from Ron and Muriel Johnson.

HEATHER GILL

This photo from June 2016 is very special to me, as it was a meal with my late best friend, before The Stag closed its doors. Denise had the pub then. From left to right is Kevin Wright, Mary Wright, Heather Gill, Graham Gill.

NETTA GLOVER

I remember going to The Stag in its heyday. What enormous fun it was. Michel was the best ever.

DAISY GOYEN

A waitress' memoir of a 92 year old fire starter!

I wanted to share a memory of mine that will last forever about one specific Sunday shift when Denise and Simon ran the pub!

It was a sunny Sunday shift must have been in 2015/2016. It was looking like a usual busy Sunday with the beautiful sound of the grand piano playing to set the ambience. We used to serve lots of customers all of whom were celebrating and enjoying time with their loved ones, families and friends.

I remember seeing a large number of people come in to celebrate a lovely lady turning 92! She was in a beautiful yellow two-piece with her hair all curled and perfectly set. She totally enjoyed her birthday meal. When it came to dessert time, Denise asked me to take her icecream to her with a candle in, and sing whilst the piano played Happy Birthday....the sound of the entire restaurant singing happy birthday was incredible and the little lady was thoroughly chuffed and felt like the queen for those few moments.

I put the dessert with the candle and flame in front of her at the table ready for her to make her wish and blow it out...but what she did instead was lean in to turn herself around to thank all the other diners for singing to her, when woahhh her hair burst into flames! Shock echoed through the entire pub, but thankfully all was ok apart from the stench of burnt hair. I remember the lady saying after her traumatic experience that she never uses hairspray, but did today as it was a special occasion!

A gentleman from a another table came over to make sure she was ok and he said to her something on the lines of 'I don't suppose you remember me but...I was here this time last year celebrating my birthday when you was celebrating yours...and I remember you choked during your birthday meal and an ambulance was called for you...!'

On her way out of the restaurant she grabbed hold of my hands and gave me a hug and said in all my years of celebrating birthdays, this will be one of my most memorable ones and told me not to worry. She also said she would think twice about wearing hairspray again and maybe the year after we should have all 3 emergency services on speed dial just in case!

CORINNE GRIFFIN

I cannot remember very much except that a lot of the jockeys who rode horses for Lord Roseberry from the Towers used to drink in the public bar.

My grandad was Percy Roper from Wing and Ivinghoe. His dad had worked as a groom for the stud and that is how he knew the jockeys.

My Mum thought he received some good racing tips over the years and made some winnings.

DEBORAH HALE-HALL

The year is 1984 when this picture was taken outside The Stag.

I remember having a glass of champagne with my sister Dee Lewis-Hall whilst waiting for the estate agents to tell me that I had completed on my first house purchase in Cheddington. What a wonderful sight to see on my first day in my new home - the hunt.

My acceptance as a "newbie" to The Stag was quick and I interacted and tried to get involved in all aspects of weekly entertainment which included on Sundays playing Spoof and eating roast potatoes which were leftovers from Michel's fabulous restaurant.

We played, and without blowing my own trumpet, I won many games of high cockalorum (leg wrestling) on the floor of the public bar including beating quite strong men.

One of my fondest memories although I appreciate maybe not for everyone was the commencement of the "Pink Nipple Cup". This was a clay pigeon trophy for men and women which we played for every year at James Henderson's farm.

Much fun was had by all and we all repaired back to The Stag for a sumptuous luncheon where the trophies were awarded. No more comments needed at this point!

Of course one of my best memories was an auction to raise money for St Mary's Church Mentmore held in the restaurant where I bid for a dinner party for 6 people cooked at home - I invited the vicar - Roger Hale to that dinner and the rest they say is history!

ANDREA HANSON

Patrick Vervoux, my husband, was a member of the ACF (Association Culinaire Française) which is based in London.

There was at the time much competition between the different restaurants in the area in the 1980s. Apart from The Stag, there was the King's Head in Ivinghoe, where Patrick and I both worked, which is where we met. The owner and our boss is still there and he is over 90 now! He is French and his name is Georges de Maison. The third restaurant was The Bell in Aston Clinton.

There were celebrities that came to the restaurant. Many businessmen who were well known in the area, but the person who was well known was Stirling Moss and his wife Susie, (they lived in nearby Tring) who came every week to have Patrick's "duck à l'orange".

Michel and Patrick would regularly entertain members of the Association Culinaire Française. Many of them were chefs in top London restaurants.

The Stag attracts a lot of nice cars, including vintage cars used on film sets and motoring clubs.

FIONA HARRISON

I have had the pleasure of entertaining the Mentmore villagers on The Green to celebrate VE Day on 8th May 2020. I have never actually been for a meal at The Stag, although it was always one of those places I wanted to visit and dine at. I only stopped there once, back in 1990. I am a diabetic and I had a hypo on my way to Tring. It was quite late and I was hoping to have dinner. It was all very spontaneous, so I hadn't booked a table, but sadly they had stopped serving and very kindly gave me some Turkish Delight, so I could resume my journey!

JAMES HENDERSON

Michel Rigal was a quite extraordinary man.

He told me that in his early twenties, during National Service, he was trained as a French paratrooper, jumping out or aircraft fully armed, on 29 occasions during exercises over Chad of all places. In those days Chad was part of French Territorial Colonies in Northern Africa, now known as the Republic of Chad since 1960.

This was taken with much amusement and leg pulling from the rabble in the public bar who gave him merciless stick for much of his many years at The Stag.

He of course was named "Froggy" and I remember a caption on the wall that read, "Bugger the lions at Longleat, have you met The Frog at Mentmore?"

There was a time in my younger day that I was friendly with a lovely young lady from Wingrave, and she kept her own horse at the bottom of her garden in a stable.

Unfortunately for her I wasn't a very punctual or reliable suitor. She knew where I was and decided to visit me on horseback at The Stag.

Well things got a little out of hand and she rode the animal through the double front doors into the public bar. Michel was in the cellar at the time and the animal was stepping about in the bar when Froggy appeared with dust all over him from the cellar stairs.

He loudly shouted at me "What is this 'orse doing in my public bar?" To which I replied, "can we have it medium rare?"

This was not the only time we had animals in the bar. When I had the agricultural contracting business, I employed seasonal workers from New Zealand who were mostly farmer's sons and good workers. We held a last bash for them in the public bar, so Lambchop (he was a butcher) and I went and rounded up some lambs on the farm, two I remember and put some frilly knickers on them and rolled a blouse around their necks with a bow tie (I think) and let them loose in the public bar as a leaving present. The Kiwis were not amused, but Froggy thought it was great. However, we had to clear the droppings.

Unbeknown to us, the local bobby a certain PC Windeler was sat unseen behind the door. He took it all in his stride.

This was what The Stag was about in the '70s and '80s all good clean fun. In the very early days when Michel took over the Stag in 1964, my father drank there and at the age of 14 years old, I had to sit outside in a very old Land Rover whilst my dad would sup ale in the bar.

Michel felt sorry for me and brought me out a packet of crisps and a bottle of coke. He did let me in occasionally when I was 15 years old and I had to sit in the corner. He always, for the next nearly three decades, reminded me of this.

I do remember when a Jack Russell jumped out of a top storey window, where the Spanish waiters lived about 30 feet up, and landed in the car park and survived.

In those early days, Helen Michel's first wife, was in the kitchens and very hard she worked. I remember my father taking a brace of pheasant up there. Helen plucked and gutted them and we ate them for supper in the restaurant that evening.

At about this time there was a young lady, a farmer's daughter. When she thought the meal was slow coming, she ate the flowers on the table and then moved around and ate all the other tables' rations.

Netty and Bob Ingles ran the bar and the cellar for many years, Netty was stern and strict and barred us all many times. She had a heart of gold when Michel came through from the kitchen and threw flour balls at us and we would retaliate and always plaster Netty. Bob was in charge of the cellar and could never understand why he always had a large brewery bill for Grolsch premium lager and not many punters drunk it but crates of empties always came up the ramp from the cellar dragged by the draymen!

Those were the days of Wild Willy Barrett on the piano in the public bar. Always on a Friday night, diners would come and admire and listen to him.

And then of course there were the blacksmiths - the Mildred brothers, who had the Forge at the bottom of Stag Hill. They were daily regulars and good job the Forge was downhill.

They had a fierce cat called Fang, which unfortunately was on Roger's car roof when he sped off to Cheddington, hence having lack of front teeth!

Roger once placed an anvil on the public bar and it stayed there for a week because Michel wasn't strong enough to move it.

A few years before Michel packed up, he took his eyes off the ball for a time and got in a bit of a mess financially.

One night I got a very worried phone call from Michel not knowing what to do and asking for my help. I raised the alarm to six good men, and we sorted him out with the help of some very bright and loyal businessmen and got him back on an even keel. But alas, he had worked so hard all his life for the benefit of others and I think he had had enough. I think this was an example of the calibre of the man that within a week or so his close friends to whom he had given so much, rallied round to help him. That says it all about the wonderful man, who I was lucky enough to call my friend.

This is a story which happened quite often, mainly in the summer, before Mentmore went on the main sewer. The septic tank from The Stag overflowed at least last twice most summers. Normally on a Sunday, when the bars and restaurant was rammed full.

Michel would ring me in a blind panic about 10.00 am on a Sunday when he came into work, to tell me that the garden and grass area where people sat, and sometimes ate, was flooded with raw sewage.

I sprang into action with various pumps, a tractor and tanker (parked on Stag Hill), then sucked out the sewage.

The smell was pretty awful, and just as the first guests arrived he was out there with a watering can and smelly disinfectant spraying the grass and hard standing. To be fair he normally paid me in food and booze.

Bernie White took his chainsaw into The Stag and started cutting table legs to make them sit evenly on the floor without rocking about, and the table leg offcuts where thrown onto the open fire.

PETE HUMPHREY

I have two paintings of No.17 The Green where my parents lived. One was given to them on their Diamond Wedding and another one when they left the village and moved to Cheddington in about 1990.

Mr Jack Nash was the landlord when I was young and when he retired Michel, a French man was the landlord. When I was 13 and 14 after school I used to bottle up for him, so I have been up and down the cellar stairs a good few times.

That handle on the door looks just the same as it did 70 years ago and I can remember how it used to sound.

Looking at The Stag picture of the porch and door brings back wonderful memories to me, I can remember sitting there having my Smiths crisps and drinking Vimto 70 years ago, while mum and dad were in the public bar.

I was born at 17 The Green in June 1944, but then the houses did not have numbers or house names - the postman knew where everybody lived.

I lived in the village with mum and dad until I was 20 then I moved to Herne Bay Kent.

Going through some of my parents old paper work and photos, I found out that Porridge Pot (near Grove Church) was owned by The Earl of Rosebery and it used to be a brickworks. They made bricks for the houses that were built in Mentmore, and they were taken from the brick works to Mentmore by horse and cart. I have so many good memories of Mentmore.

Top left to right, uncles Ernie and Len, my dad, George, Fred, Bert. Bottom row Auntie Doris, Grandad, Grandmother and Auntie Nell. Photo taken at Porridge Pot.

My birthplace, No. 17 The Green.

DAVID HUTTON-POTTS

This remarkable photo is of my father Jack Hutton-Potts doing his famous "egg trick". A tin bar tray is placed on top of a pint mug of water or beer. A match box, minus its drawer and matches, is placed on its side in the middle of the tray. A raw egg is placed on top of the match box. The tray is then struck briskly from one side. When the trick is successfully done the egg lands unbroken in the glass. Needless to say Michel Rigal had to get the carpet cleaned when the trick went wrong!

On his way to achieving a Michelin star for The Stag Inn restaurant, Michel Rigal used to purchase his meat as a whole side of beef and he would do his own butchery. One day, when walking across The Green to visit Dorothy and Elaine, I saw Bruno, Dorothy's Labrador-cross dog dragging down the road what appeared to be the remains of half a cow which he had retrieved from The Stag dustbins back home to eat at his leisure. Fortunately I was able to warn Dorothy of the impending unwanted "gift"!

I was briefly a member of the Sotheby's portering team whilst they were cataloguing the contents of the Towers in 1977.

A selection of photos of regulars at The Stag in 1973.

ROSIE KNIGHT

On March 17th 1997 we moved to Mentmore and first entered the pub to find it in a time warp, The Christmas tree and some decorations were still left in the public bar, not a needle left on the tree! A feeling of fighting through cobwebs came to mind. A new manager had only recently taken over and the locals were anticipating great things.

Friday nights became play nights with soda syphon fights and leg wrestling matches. A dishy (!) chef arrived from the Cotswolds working only for long weekends. His job was to enhance the restaurant with some culinary delights, but financially it didn't work.

Then Will and Mandy arrived from Berkhamsted Golf Club, having previously managed the Club House. He was a good chef but we got the feeling they wished they were somewhere else. His passion was flying and he had a part share in a plane so would take off when he could!

Thursday nights were also skiffle nights with Wild Willy Barrett from the Old Grey Whistle Test who was in charge along with a throng of locals who would provide great entertainment, the drinkers joining in dancing (some on tables)! Until we were thrown out.

Sunday night also was a regular music night with a temporary stage erected in the restaurant, different guests sang on various happy occasions in various dress modes.

Will and Mandy left and Norman Wisdom made a bid for The Stag. He made several visits to discuss furnishings for the pub but on the due date for signing with the brewery he failed to show up! Eventually Mike (chef) and Jenny Tuckwood were appointed. Mike had an army officers mess background and refused to cook chips, which he was constantly barraged about!

What a social period! Dinner events were held most months with themed dressing-up to suit the occasion and wine flowing with good food. People came in taxis from afar as it became very popular.

On a personal note Mike and Jenny were very kind. Mike arrived at my home the night my husband passed away (61) to say they would be organising the wake at The Stag to take away additional stress. Large numbers came and no charge was made, also no chips were served! My husband was an offender!

They left due to the high rent the brewery were charging.

Mark Webber racing driver and Anne his partner took over with a complete makeover of The Stag; an Italian theme. What a change, lots or rumblings in the Mentmore jungle. However Mark Webber's frequent appearances at The Stag provided lots of friendly chats about the motor racing world etc. and the pizzas were very popular.

Nigel Bradshaw was bought in as manager who tried to re-introduce social events. The Webber period finished due to lack of profit and high rent.

There were periods in the early days when the pub was left without anyone to run it. However the locals, mainly fronted by Nicky Belton who had worked behind the bar, worked hard to keep the doors open so the locals could still meet up. She kept the kitchen open with good old basic egg and chips etc. so the camaraderie continued and drinking flourished.

These are just a few thoughts of times that I can remember, lots of them were in an alcoholic haze! Without the pub I would have had a very unhappy existence after Ian died. It was a place where we made many friends, so I felt very happy to go there on my own to meet them.

THE LANGLEY FAMILY

No.25 The Green, Mentmore, since 1981 had been the home of the Langley family. Although I moved to Hampshire 3 years ago, I still miss the community spirit of Mentmore.

A whole generation of Mentmore children spent their formative years in and out of that house either being child-minded by me or playing with those who were. The house holds many happy memories for those children (now adults).

I was a childminder for 20 years and a nanny for 10 years and still keep in contact with the children I cared for.

We lived in the shop and Post Office. The Old Forge, which was next door, we made into part of the house in 1985/6. When the telephone box was removed from the front garden it had to be lifted out by a crane.

The Village Hall and The Green were given to the community by Lady Rosebery and administered by the Parish Council on behalf of the community.

I remember knocking on people's doors to ask for volunteers to help get the Village Hall renovated as it had become so run down.

I have always been a keen gardener and had an allotment opposite the Stable Yard.

I worked for the then owners of Mentmore Towers, The Yogi Mahesh Maharishi Transcendental Meditation Movement, planting their bedding plants for several years. In the summer I would take the children for picnics in the grounds of Mentmore Towers.

The playground on The Green was instigated by me, by raising funds with barn dances etc.

I can remember Ernest and Bill Pennell who lived at Cheddington Lodge. George Pennell and his wife Peggy lived at Stone Lodge. Peggy worked at Liberty's making curtains.

With the former workshops next door to the Old Post Office, the building always had a secret – what appeared to be a domestic property at the front, at the rear was partly a blacksmith's forge.

The building formed part of a once busy complex known as the Estate Yard. From here worked not only the village carpenters, but a plumber, blacksmith, bricklayers, painters and later an electrician – all these men kept the Estate functioning and in trim, manicured condition.

Jonathan Langley putting the Christmas Tree up on The Green.

STELLA MARSHALL WRITTEN BY ROBERT ADAMS

Like many of us, I was very sad to read that Stella Marshall from Ledburn had died. Her family was connected to the Mentmore Estate for over a hundred years, and Stella had recorded many of her village memories on both paper and tape. I think it would be good to remember her here as she typified many of the people born on the Estate and a way of life which is now gone for ever. So with the help of Stella's niece, Rose Norton, here are some photos and a potted biography, but more importantly one of the small booklets she wrote about her childhood in Mentmore as a separate post above.

Stella was born Stella Elizabeth Norton on 7 February 1924 in Ashington, Northumberland, to Robert and Constance Norton (nee Jacobs). When Stella was about 18 months old the family came to Mentmore where her mother became the village postmistress and ran the village shop while her father worked on the estate. The family already had long-time connections to Mentmore; her grandparents Emily and George Jacobs lived at the Gas House; George was in charge of the gas production which powered the village – although electricity had been installed at the mansion around 1900 – Stella's Great Uncle George was the village electrician.

Eventually, Stella joined her older brother, Philip, at Mentmore School, but was really happiest when amongst her extended family in the village. Stella's great grandmother, Elizabeth Janes, her aunt and mother were founder members of Mentmore Women's Institute in the late 1920s with Eva, Countess of Rosebery as the first president. Stella and her younger sister, Sheila, feature prominently in many of the earlier WI photos.

After leaving school, aged 14, Stella worked briefly in the clothing industry before going into domestic service at Mentmore for Lord and Lady Rosebery; she soon swapped this for a job working for the blind MP, Captain Sir Ian Fraser and his family, who were then living at Mentmore Vicarage. When she turned 18 in 1943, she joined the Auxiliary Territorial Service where she served for over three years. She loved this time of her life, becoming a store keeper in the Royal Army Ordnance Corps.

During the war, the Norton family left the Post Office and moved to the Stud Cottage where they reported ghostly happenings! A long-dead stud groom would walk across the garden, this would precede a member of the family being killed. It must have been some relief to move to the Laundry Cottage and after a short while to the Old House in Ledburn (today called Longfields).

After being demobbed, Stella went back into domestic service, working first as a nanny and then as a cook. It was while working at Cuckfield Park, Sussex, that she met the love of her life, Harry Marshall. They were married at St Mary the Virgin, Mentmore, in 1961 with a reception at the Hare and Hounds. They then worked as a butler and cook team. Her favourite memory was working at Mereworth Castle during the filming of Casino Royale and not realising that dogs savaging an actor were not part of the plot until an ambulance arrived.

The couple's last job was as caretakers to St. Barnabas Church. In 1978, they retired and moved to their bungalow in Ledburn, next door to Stella's widowed mother. There, they became great friends with Freddy Manning, who was Lady Rosebery's retired chauffeur and long-time estate driver. Harry died in 1989 and Stella remained in Ledburn and wrote several memoirs relating to the village and estate. One of which about her childhood is reproduced here. Shortly before her death, she went to live with her niece, Rose, in Leighton Buzzard. She died August 2020 aged 96.

THE
CHANGING SCENE

The Story of a Village

from the 1920s.

STELLA MARSHALL

The Changing Scene

"All things bright and beautiful" sang the children in the little village school at Mentmore in those pre-war years. The children's hymn was a good description for Mentmore was beautiful, with an army of people to keep it so. The village of Mentmore, together with the hamlets of Ledburn and Crafton, formed the private estate of the Earl of Rosebery. The children singing were the sons and daughters of the employees who lived in the tied cottages on the estate.

Although there was great unemployment in the country no-one was unemployed on the estate because, as soon as a man gave notice to leave his job, he would be given notice to leave his home, ready for his replacement.

In charge of the estate was the Agent who lived in the Manor House at Ledburn. Under his direction were a Head Gardener, a Head Groom at the riding stables near the church, another Head Groom at the race-horse stud and a groom in charge of the yearling stud at Crafton.

The large house in the centre of Mentmore, next to the post office, was the workshop for the use of the maintenance workers. This building had a frontage to give the impression that it was a residential building but, although it had an upper floor, it was really just a shell for the use of the two carpenters, the plumber, two painters, the bricklayers and labourers. There was a stable at the back for a cart horse. This horse was put out on the village green on summer evenings for then the green was completely enclosed by iron railings about four feet high. These railings were taken for scrap metal for the war effort at the beginning of the war and were not replaced afterwards. The building to the left of the workshop was the blacksmith's forge. All the work on the estate was done with horses for there were no tractors then, it was all carthorses which were brought to the blacksmith and his assistant to be shod. There were racks of iron rails at the back of the forge which were made into horseshoes and for railings around the fields which were partly hidden by hedges and trees.

To the left of the forge was the village shop and post office. Sweets, cigarettes and some groceries were sold here. There was an old-style upright telephone on the counter and the Head Gardener and Head Groom made their calls from it. Only Lord Rosebery, his agent, the district nurse and the vicar had private phones. In the late thirties, a phone box was put outside but was moved onto the green in later years. The postman called each day for the mail which had been franked by the postmistress. At Christmas, cards could be sent for less postage if the envelope was only tucked in and not sealed. People sent poultry by post, with all the feathers on and a strong label tied to the bird's legs. The birds were left lying on the floor in the shop until the postman collected them in the van. He used a bicycle at other times.

On Saturdays, the children were given their pocket-money - their Saturday half-penny or penny. A half-penny would buy two ounces of sweets such as humbugs, bullseyes, toffees, dolly mixtures or a bag of sherbet. The postmistress would weigh the sweets on small brass scales and put the sweets into small white paper bags.

The children may not have had much pocket-money then but they did have plenty of places to play. There was the green and the fields which only contained animals and were not used for crops so it was possible to go a long way across the fields, whether on the rights of way or not. The little girls thought nothing of walking half-a-mile to a spinney to pick the wild violets which grew there and then walk back again.

Children were not given the amount of toys that today's children have but they had one great advantage - they had plenty of opportunity to use and develop an imagination. The toys were very basic - a doll's pram was not a smaller edition of a baby's pram but was made very simply. Christmas was looked forward to and enjoyed so much more than at present. Children were told that their parents could not afford several expensive presents and this was true. There was no television to advertise luxuries. Some presents were home-made, it was cheaper to buy a doll wearing a simple cotton covering and then for the mother or aunt to make clothes for it. Christmas was the one time of the year for a present, a birthday one was just something small if at all.

The quiet country roads were safe then for children. There was hardly any traffic, sometimes we would meet only one car on a Sunday evening family walk to Bridego Bridge. Sometimes there would be gypsies camping there, genuine gypsies with horse-drawn caravans and campfires. They always left the site tidy and never left rubbish. Another walk was to Ledburn, the brook there was popular with the children for paddling in. Ledburn and Mentmore also had a tennis court but there are cottages there now. The little chapel at Ledburn was well attended as was the mediaeval church at Mentmore.

There had been a chapel at Mentmore but it had been extended and converted into a school by Hannah de Rothschild in the nineteenth century. In the mid nineteenth century, Amschel de Rothschild bought Mentmore, Ledburn and Crafton to create a country estate, it passed to Hannah who married the Earl of Rosebery. She re-arranged the village and it has come to be known as her village but in reality Mentmore had existed for centuries. It was also a Roman burial ground.

In the school were three dolls in glass cases, dressed in nineteenth century clothes, one as a little girl in a red cloak, one as a boy and the other in grey to represent a governess, depicting the uniform of that time. The governess doll was broken but the other two are now in the County Museum at Aylesbury.

At the bottom of the Stag Hill was the dairy with the Home Farm behind it. The dairy was a very attractive place with well-kept lawns all round it and pink japonica growing on the walls and on a pergola which led to the estate gardens. On the lawns were peacocks but these were sent to Whipsnade Zoo at the beginning of the war.

The milk was brought from the farm every morning and afternoon and was on sale at 8 a.m. and 4 p.m. A farm labourer, wearing a wooden yoke on his shoulders, would carry two large pails of milk attached to the yoke by chains, from the farm to the dairy. Some was then put through a machine which separated the cream from the milk. Some cream was made into butter which, with the rest of the cream, would be sent to the kitchen of his lordship's house. It was the children's job to fetch the milk for their mothers who could buy a pint of new (straight from the cow) milk for 2d (two old pence) or 2 pints of separated milk for 1d.

School ended at 4 p.m. and the children would run home to collect their milk cans which were usually of white enamel with a blue rim and which held about 2-3 pints. Some children collected milk for people who had no children and were given a few coppers each week for doing so.

There were two teachers and thirty children from four to fourteen years although the official age to start school was five. The under-sevens were called infants and their's was a more relaxed atmosphere but, for the older ones, it was "Sit still and no talking." After hours of this, 4 o'clock was the time to let rip, running down the hill, collecting your milk then walking back up that steep hill. This usually included the game of swinging the cans backards and forwards, then in a complete circle. The trick was to keep your elbow straight, forget and the lid would come off, spilling the milk. Never mind, run back and get a refill and also a telling-off from the dairymaid.

In those pre-war days, Mentmore Towers was always called just Mentmore, never the Towers and to the estate people it was always "the mansion". A huge Victorian building, it housed a large number of domestic servants. In the back drive was the private laundry with resident laundrymaids and at the entrance to the back drive was the nightwatchman's lodge.

Opposite the church was the large Victorian vicarage where lived the vicar with his crippled wife whom he took on his rounds in her bathchair. The vicar employed a cook, a maid and a gardener. He was only in charge of Mentmore church then and did not have Cheddington and Mareworth as at the present time.

There were two chauffeurs living near the church to drive his lodship's cars which were kept in large garages at the bottom of the hill. At that time, all cars were black, as were all bicycles and metal prams. Most of the villagers rode bikes for there was no other transport until a bus service from Tring to Leighton Buzzard was started in the Thirties and then there were three or four buses every day. The driver and conductor wore uniform with peaked caps. It took twenty minutes to go to Leighton Buzzard from Mentmore. On the return journey, the bus could only just get up the Big Hill but, when the Womens Institute hired a charabanc (coach) to go on an outing, it couldn't make it over a hump-backed bridge near Cheddington and all the women had to get out and walk over the bridge.

The older children used to cycle to the Oriel Cinema in Leighton Buzzard (now a supermarket). It was quite safe to leave their bikes in the racks provided behind the cinema during the three hour programme. They paid 3d (three old pence) each for seats in the front row.

There were no police panda cars, just ordinary black saloon cars and we used to see the men cleaning them outside the police station in Mentmore Road, Linslade. The estate was under the care of a constable who lived in the village of Cheddington 1½ miles away. He would come around on his cycle with his cape folded and laid over his shoulder and bicycle clips on his trousers. His tunic was buttoned right up to the neck. He was known as "the bobby" and the boys said they were "frit (frightened) to death of him". If he caught them in mischief he would tell their dads, for he knew everyone on his beat and that almost guaranteed a good hiding. No-one bothered with juvenile courts.

The adult courts dealt much more severely with law-breakers. Murderers were hanged, hooligans birched and there was flogging in prisons.

There was no television and radio was only just beginning. My father had one, known as a "cat's whisker" and the slightest movement lost the sound but later he had a large polished wireless and we would listen to Uncle Mac on "Children's Hour". Children were not allowed to use an adult's Christian name unless it included aunt or uncle so we all had a lot of unoffical relations.

There was no electricity in the village at one time. the wireless ran on a large battery and oil lamps and candles were used for lighting and the old-style blackleaded kitchen ranges for cooking.

At one end of the road at Mentmore is the old village pump which supplied water to ten cottages. The women used to fetch the water in white enamelled pails for all purposes. The post office and two other cottages shared one tap in the backyard. The blacksmithh used to thaw it out in winter. The two cottages near the village hall had one tap between them. For washing, everyone had a galvanised bath, to be filled and emptied by hand. Even so, it seemed to be a healthy life, all produce was organic and eggs were free-range. They were sold by the score (20) or half-score at Rowden Farm.

The district nurse lived in one of the cottages near the pump. A doctor only called for serious illnesses, the nurse delivered the babies and cared for people over quite a wide area, making her rounds in her little black Austin car. We didn't seem to hear so much about cancer then. The dreaded ailment then was TB, called consumption. The treatment was a long stay in a special hospital and lots of fresh air. Pneumonia was also a killer disease. Children would be told "You'll catch your death of cold" if they got wet.

Winter was a delight for the children when there was snow but this was not popular with the grownups. There were no cars or gritting lorries to keep the roads clear and if a cart went along the road it would make ridges which would freeze, making it difficult to walk or cycle on.

The Countess used to give the schoolchildren a party at Christmas in the school. Each child could choose a gift to the value of half-a-crown and the senior teacher would do the shopping for them. A large tree was brought in from the estate and decorated by the teachers. There was also a bag of sweets, an apple and an orange for each child. A half-crown was two shillings and sixpence and would buy a doll or a book or paints etc. The men's wages were about thirty shillings a week at one time.

Autumn was also pleasant with plenty of blackberries to pick to make pies, jam or wine. Most of the villagers made wine with sloes, dandelions, cowslips, elderberries etc. It was made in a large earthenware tub with a piece of toast with yeast on it floating on the top. Crab apples made jelly and most people grew some fruit in their gardens. The children collected conkers to play with. Their usual toys were tops, hoops, skipping ropes and dolls but none of the sophisticated toys of today.

In summer, the little girls liked to watch the haymaking at the farm at the bottom of the Stag Hill. The hay was all turned by hand and collected up into carts and taken to the place where the ricks were made, using an escalator to take the hay to the top of the rick. The escalator was turned by a horse walking in a circle. The carts would go to the fields empty and the children were given a ride there, walking back beside the horse.

In the spring there were violets, cowslips and ladysmocks to pick. There were lambs in the fields. All farms were mixed, with sheep, cattle, pigs, hes and, of course, the horses. The men worked longer hours but at a gentler pace, there wasn't the stress of today. Factories worked a basic 48 hour week from 8-6 and until 12.30 on Saturdays and the shops were open till late. The market stalls in Leighton Buzzard High Street had gas flares and didn't close until about 8.30-9.p.m. on Saturdays. There used to be animals in pens in the High Street just before Christmas for the Fat Stock Show.

Goods were delivered from shops, there were no supermarkets or self-service. Groceries, bread and meat were delivered to the villages. A man used to come from Wing with ice-cream in a special little cart drawn by a pony and ring a handbell to let the people know he was there. The children would run home for a half-penny for a small cornet and the mothers would give them a plate to bring some back for the grown-ups. No-one had fridges, just a cold larder and a meat safe - a small metal cupboard with perforated sides and door to allow air in but which kept flies out.

It seemed as if that way of life would go on for ever. We didn't realise how life was gradually changing. No-one in those pre-war years could ever have believed that the estate would not always belong to his lordship and that one day it would be sold but that is what did happen in what came to be known as the "Sale of the Century" on the 18th-27th May 1977. The treasures from the mansion were auctioned and the building sold. The cottages are no longer tied cottages but privately owned.

The hedges are a fraction of their previous height and some have gone completely to make larger fields for growing crops. The big wood has gone and the mixed farms have become either arable or dairy farms. The racehorse stud and the riding stables were sold and the buildings converted for residential use. The village school was closed and sold. No-one collects milk from the dairy anymore.

The "Stag" public house at Mentmore and the "Hare and Hounds" at Ledburn were sold. Both have been altered inside and enlarged but are not changed a great deal at the front of the buildings.

At Mentmore, the mediaeval church is still used for the purpose for which it was built. Let us hope that it continues to do so!

ROBERT MILDRED

Roger Mildred, the village blacksmith, the drinker, the jovial character, the man with many skills and a heart of gold... my dad.

His main craft was a blacksmith, but could turn his hand to almost anything. He featured in books, demonstrated his skills at local farm open days and gave talks in schools.

When I was sixteen I worked alongside him in the Forge, but I was more interested in motor cars and went into that trade instead of following in his footsteps.

Mentmore Towers estate was enclosed by nine miles of iron fencing, which gave the Blacksmith plenty of work to do carrying out repairs.

As well as the day to day, shoeing of horses, making and repairing agricultural and household implements etc. he produced decorative wrought iron work both inside and outside The Stag pub.

I was always astounded at how after drinking eight beers at lunchtime he could then go back to work and make intricate ironwork within 1mm precision.

The gates below are at Hoggeston Church, near Winslow. The gate was commissioned from Roger Mildred to commemorate the Micklem family who lived at Mains Hill. Robert (Bob) Micklem was a regular at The Stag until his premature and sudden death, aged 29, in 1980. A stag was their family crest.

It was well known in the village that my dad ran The Stag " from the other side of the bar". With his vibrant, full of life, sense of humour and amazing personality, everyone he met would warm to him immediately. The

antics he got up to were second to none. Michel Rigal, of course, was a good mate and was asked to be my godfather which he proudly accepted.

You will have realised by now, that my dad loved his beer, and it was the social life that he enjoyed in The Stag too - 14 times a week for 14 years.

He was very well known by all the locals and he would generously help his fellow neighbours in any way he could and, of course, buy them a pint or two.

My dad had many parties at the Forge over the years. He would cover tables with wallpaper and sellotape and provide ham hocks, cheeses and chutneys and obviously a barrel of beer.

Of course, the Forge was used for many other activities as the above photo shows him plucking a pheasant.

Another story I remember is of when he was drinking in The Stag and got invited to a friend's house and they ended up drinking a bottle of whiskey there. His friend said he could get his horse to sit on command. Dad said "OK let's see it then" so they got the horse from the paddock and led him in through the front door into the sitting room. By tickling the horses back flanks, the horse just sat there with his bottom on the floor and his front legs out straight on the carpet, while the men proceeded to drink the rest of the bottle.

When he was fitting a replacement bell in the bell tower of Mentmore Church, he realised he needed some extra help with lifting the bell. He saw three people out for a stroll and asked them if they could lend some muscle power to help. Of course they were persuaded to do so by later enjoying a couple of pints of filthy foaming ale at The Stag.

I was standing at the pub window when my dad shouted to Michel "there's no alcohol here Kermi". Michel replied "right oh Roger" and Michel got a bottle of whiskey and lobbed it over the road to The Forge where Roger ran down the driveway and caught it!

In the 1980s he kidnapped his mate Alan Jones. Alan's wife was in on the kidnap and had secretly packed a holdall for her husband. Dad said he was taking him out for the evening, and in the van, much to his surprise eight of their mates were hiding there. However, when Alan realised they had been driving for over five hours, he knew this was not a local jaunt. They ended up driving all the way to Cornwall visiting the sole surviving Tamar sailing barge the "Shamrock" for a few days and yes, you guessed it, drinking more beer in the back of the van.

In the 1990s my dad lived on a narrow boat, which he named "Pops" as a dedication to his mother.

The other side to my dad was his caring nature and helping others as much as he could.

He even spent time in Africa building two schools and funding a bore hole to be dug so the people of Botswana had fresh water.

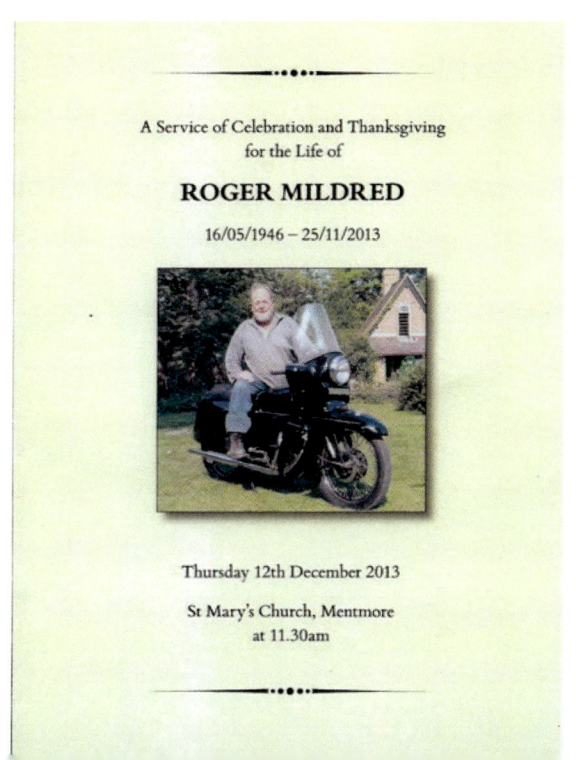

A Service of Celebration and Thanksgiving
for the Life of

ROGER MILDRED

16/05/1946 – 25/11/2013

One African family were invited to come to Mentmore and you guessed it, they went to The Stag for a drink.

Thursday 12th December 2013

So, cheers Dad ... this one's for you.

St Mary's Church, Mentmore
at 11.30am

NAN MORRISON

Michel was always a gentleman and manners were everything to him. His knowledge of the English language and his crossword skills were amazing. He always had a twinkle in his eye and wonderful sense of humour.

Michel worked very hard and long hours, but he loved his life at Mentmore and nothing was too much trouble for him.

PAUL O'CARROLL

We took some friends to The Stag one evening and mentioned that it was owned by Mark Webber.

One of our party was dismissive, saying many pubs were owned by celebrities, but they rarely showed a face or took any interest.

Shortly after we were seated at our table, there was a slight commotion at the door as two gentlemen came in. I was quietly pleased to see the first of the two men was Mark Webber... But was even happier when I saw the second man was none other than Jackie Stewart.

DIANE PAYNE

The Stable Yard was a big part of our lives and we were proud of what we created. Terry myself and our two teenage children Colin and Paula moved to Mentmore in 1978, and purchased The Stable Yard.

We sold a part to Terry's brother, house and office and stables attached and they renovated their part and we renovated ours. The coach houses (state coaches were kept there during the war) granary/stable block indoor riding school and the main house, yes a lot of hard work (something we all had never been afraid of).

So, what it became was a lovely place to live and work and a lovely place for people to come to, B&B coach house

THE PROPERTY

The Stable Yard, built 150 years ago in the historic village of Mentmore by the 5th Earl of Roseberry, has been redeveloped as a fascinating complex.

Sited around a beautiful cobbled courtyard you will find the licensed Restaurant and Craft Gallery, a Beauty Room, bed and breakfast accommodation, and the recently completed Conference Room.

The Bed and Breakfast accommodation, which is registered with the English Tourist Board, comprises of four unique, individually decorated bedrooms and a suite of rooms (originally the Groom's rooms), all have en-suite facilities.

guest rooms and in the stables, a craft gallery, tea rooms and beauty room, and lots of lovely local girls working with me. We did this for several years, it's a long time ago now.

I'm a great grandma now and I've been living in Normandy for over 14 years just about to move to an apartment and retire (age 76) after running a B&B in my home.

What was so lovely was the times we all met up at The Stag to relax after a hard day's work as so many of us newcomers were renovating our lovely old houses. The old folks told us about their life working for The Rosebery family. We sat around the piano singing songs and made lovely new friends and we still meet up and keep in touch.

Last but not least, "The Lovely Stag", what a wonderful place and the landlord Michel was a lovely man who had so many friends and he had time for everyone. I am so pleased I was one of his friends and, like so many people, loved and respected him. He will never be forgotten. I wish the new owners of The Stag all the best wishes for the years to come.

KATE AND KEN PAYNE

Ken and Kate moved to the head groom's house in Mentmore in 1978.

At that time The Stable Yard was enclosed with massive oak gates at the entrance and the Granary can still be seen today.

Next to their house was the stable office, with the tack room and stables in the square courtyard. The Stable Yard had its own indoor riding school and the Pony Club met there.

The hunt was a weekly event. The hounds were kennelled at Ascott House and the horses and hounds would pass by their house, taking up the whole road.

On Ken's 50th birthday they had a party in a field they own with a marquee and hog roast. Ken remembers when Malcolm Osborne the vicar at Mentmore Church came into The Stag and asked for some help lifting the "Hatchment" (coat of arms) in the church. Roger Mildred had made a chain for it to hang and the men balanced on old pieces of wood as scaffolding to lift it up.

The Thursday Club held at The Stag began when all the local tradesmen would meet to pay their labourers.

The Thursday Club also held shooting parties and Michel would make game pies for all of them.

The Harvest Supper was for the local farmers at the end of the season. Michel would cater for over 100 people sitting at long tables serving roast beef dinners and plentiful "seconds".

One Christmas, The Stag was fully booked with diners, but some of the people couldn't hear the singing and music playing on the piano in the public bar. Michel decided the piano would have to be moved! He got all the lads to lift the piano over the bar and into the dining area so everyone could enjoy the singsong.

Manuel and his wife worked at The Stag, but when it was really busy Manuel would leave the pub and take any bicycle that was outside and go for a ride around the village. When his frustration had simmered he would come back and continue his work.

One Saturday lunch time, Roger Mildred decided to auction a bale of hay at the pub. The bale of hay was taken from a truck outside in the car park. He brought it in and auctioned split up sections of the bale. The straw went everywhere!

Michel was loved by everyone and he was very generous! When it was Kate's birthday, they went to The Stag for dinner and as it was her birthday she ordered the best on the menu – lobster. Michel insisted that they shouldn't pay for the meal as she was the birthday girl, but Kate was also insistent and bought him a bottle of whiskey (coals to Newcastle).

THE STABLE YARD
Craft Gallery

Mentmore, near Leighton Buzzard, Bedfordshire LU7 0QG.

A fascinating selection of original hand-crafted work from all over Britain will be displayed in the unique setting of the Old Stables, built 150 years ago by the Fifth Earl of Rosebery.

Among the craft for sale at a wide range of prices will be –

POTTERY OF ALL KINDS
BASKETRY
PATCHWORK
TURNED WOOD ITEMS
WOODEN PUZZLES AND TOYS
DRIED FLOWERS
BLOWN AND STAINED GLASS
SOFT TOYS AND DOLLS

All displayed to their best advantage on renovated furniture which will also be for sale.

Open Wednesday – Sunday: 10 a.m. – 6 p.m.

AMPLE CAR PARKING

The Craft Gallery Flyer.

Ken Payne, Kate Payne, June Wiggins enjoying a summer's evening at The Stag.

Kate Payne sitting on carved bench made by Les Langley.

TERRY PAYNE

I would not know where to start as so much went on in the front bar when Froggy (Michel) had the pub. To give you some idea... sheep in the bar with bra and knickers on, a horse that we could not get back out, a wife coming in the bar with her husband's Sunday dinner and smashing it down on the table, Froggy putting a water hose though the window and spraying the customers with water, and a piano stuck behind the bar so that Wild Willy Barratt could play it in the restaurant.

Old Tom Compton used to come in The Stag with his two Scottie dogs. If a stranger made a fuss of them he would always say in a sad voice, "got a 'ave 'em put down t'morra as can't afford to keep 'em." He was loaded, always came in for his bullock sandwich as he called a steak sandwich. Just one of the old characters.

One New Year's Eve, Rodney Johnson was playing his bagpipes when he ran out of breath. Michel got a gas cylinder out of the cellar, connected it to the bagpipes and turned it on - one big bang and the bag split wide open! This was a very expensive laugh, but all in good fun.

IAN PERRY

Unsure exactly when, but around 1981, I went to The Stag with my wife Lesley and friends Angela and Adam Chandler on a birthday treat. We had always been told it was "the place to go and was posh".

With the men all dressed up in jacket and ties and the ladies impeccably attired, we entered the restaurant and went to the bar to order drinks and the Maître d' delivered menus to peruse.

At this point, we were verbally accosted by a senior gentleman and lady at the next table saying "I hope you have brought lots of money to eat in the restaurant as it costs a lot of money," in an un-joking way. Being on best behaviour, as young 25 year old can be, we gave a gentle rebuff along the lines of "we would not be here if we could not afford it". We were called through to the restaurant shortly after.

Being mid 1980s, it was still very much the time of prawn cocktail starters. A couple of us ordered one. As I pealed the top sauce and lettuce leaf away, I discovered a very substantial blow fly lying dead in the prawns.

Calling the Maître d' over...
"I seem to have a fly in my cocktail."
"Would Sir like another one?"
"No thanks, one is quite enough."

RICHARD PHILLIPS

As a neighbour, at the Manor House, we have fond memories of the legendary Michel... we used to supply him with surplus vegetables (he particularly welcomed artichokes) in return for receiving my courier-delivered papers (pre-internet days) when we were out.

DENISE REDDING AND SIMON SPARROW

I first started work at The Stag in September 1981. It was my first proper job when I left catering college. I was one of 3 or 4 new members of staff as a lot of the Spanish staff that worked there had just left (I think to set up their own place but I'm not sure). We all "lived in" but the rooms above the pub were full so I had a room at Mrs Bathurst's house (big house overlooking The Green). I believe Mrs Bathurst used to help Michel with the bookwork.

I was so chuffed to get the job, The Stag was one of the big three in the area (the other two being The King's Head at Ivinghoe and The Bell Inn at Aston Clinton) These were top places to eat out with fabulous reputations. I was to be paid £120.00 a week. This was a really good wage as all my living expenses were paid for. We worked five and a half days a week.

I have very happy memories of working at The Stag, but my goodness it was hard work! June (Sharp, now Davies) and I had to be in work for 9.30am and it was our job to make the desserts for the sweet trolley and any salad dressings/Marie Rose sauce etc., so we would be in the kitchen until 11.30 ish (there were three other chefs at the time and this was before the kitchen extension). After this we would get changed ready to work the lunch shift. Pedro (one of only two Spanish workers left) would spend the morning silver dipping all the cutlery and laying the tables (best linen of course). Eduardo was the other Spanish employee and he washed up... a very thankless task as everything had to be done by hand as there was no dishwasher.

Lunch was nearly always full. Mostly businessmen with accounts who all had their regular tables (woe betide if someone else was sat on "their" table!). Grundfos, Lancer Boss, Redland Roof and lots of others would all have lunch every day during the week.

The Stag did an à la carte menu all the time and a table d`hôte menu at weekday lunch times only. Often lunch would finish at 4.30-5.00pm we would relay the tables take a quick break and be back for evening service which started at 7.00pm. During the week it was a little quieter but at the weekend it was crazy busy with around 70 covers (people).

Michel would never turn away a regular customer, so we would often relay a table at 9-9.30pm for guests that were waiting in the lounge. Rarely would we finish before midnight and more often 1.00am. Sundays "half day" was us only working 9.30am-6.30pm! Needless to say, apart from getting my washing done, I slept most of my day off. This, of course, had its benefits in that we never had time to spend our wages so

June, Simon & Sue (head chef and barperson long before "my" Simon came along) and myself were all able to secure mortgages and buy our first homes!

There were winter nights when the snow would prevent any customers getting up "Stag Hill" and Michel would lose a day's trading. As most of us "lived in" we would sit in the lounge around the fire having a drink and telling stories. Regardless of the weather Michel managed to get to work in his green Capri. One snowy evening he offered to take me back to Wing with him (my parents lived in Wing at the time), so we set off, only to get stuck on the road between the crossroads and park gate. There was no way the Capri was going any further so we walked to Wing together.

I remember, when Simon and I were doing our business plan for The Stag, factoring in that we could lose a lot of business if we had a harsh winter. In the three years we were there it never happened.

Customers knew Michel would find them a table so, often, when told we were full, they would demand to speak to Michel. We would have to go upstairs to the top of the pub where he had his office and tell him someone wanted to speak to him. He would do the funny little growl he did when he was not amused and come downstairs to the phone (there was no way of transferring the call at the time). Very quietly he would write down a name somewhere on the diary to remind himself that they were coming, but not where we (or the chefs) would look as he knew we were full and couldn't fit anyone else in. Then he would act surprised when they turned up! On his way back up to the office he would mumble & grumble about it only being someone who wanted to book a table and why couldn't we deal with it... many years later I would laugh when the same thing would happen to me, I would like to say that I was firmer and didn't take any more bookings when we were full, but I cannot tell a lie!

Dining out at The Stag was quite an extravagance. Drinks in the lounge before dinner, wine with the meal and always a liqueur with coffee and a cigar of course. It was not "upselling" to offer a liqueur or port with coffee....it was the norm, very rarely did anyone refuse.

Smoking throughout was common place. Everything was silver service so we would be leaning over customers to serve them, or pouring their coffee while they were smoking. I have never smoked and would master the art of taking a deep breath in before I approached the table and hoping I could last until

I had finished (it was never going to happen when I had to silver serve vegetables to a table of six though ha-ha).

Guerdon work is "cooking at the table" which Michel would do (or us occasionally); crêpes Suzette, steak tartare, portioning the whole duck and taking a Dover sole off the bone were all done in front of the customer. Michel once went to take a Dover sole off the bone and it slipped into the cutlery drawer of the dumb waiter. He simply closed the drawer with the fish in it and ordered another to be brought from the kitchen!

Michel had an impressive wine cellar and port selection (looking back I have no idea how he sourced such a selection as there is no way Charles Wells stocked those items). He used to keep some of his best wines and ports in the restaurant. Roger Mildred made a wine rack which went on top of the little partition by the steps down into the lower restaurant (which is where the double gates (also made by Roger) used to be. If Michel went to get a bottle from there you knew guests were spending money! You cannot imagine the reaction from Michel when a cleaner at the time happily told him how she had given it all a good clean and got rid of "all that dust on those bottles".

We had very little to do with "the bar" as there were always designated bar staff. Walking through from the kitchen occasionally to get tap water was about all the contact we had. Michel would often walk through behind the bar to get from the kitchen to the lounge (where he took the orders) invariably heckling would ensue on both sides. It always amazed me how he could interact with the bar customers (usually involving bad language on both sides) and then seconds later become the perfect French maître d'.

It was a wonderful lesson for me to learn I'm sure you will be told various stories of happenings in the bar. Practical jokes would abound! Roger Mildred asked Michel for some wood for the fire and when it wasn't forthcoming he got a chainsaw and cut up a bar chair! Roger also once brought a horse into the bar! There would often be singsongs with Wild Willy Barrett on piano and Rodney playing the tea chest and a washboard was played along with spoons of course.

It was a place where a lot of the men that had bought properties in the big estate sale would agree to help each other with different jobs, sharing their skills and creating bonds that were to last a lifetime.

In the early '80s, The Stag (both bar & restaurant) was a very chauvinistic place where it was obvious our role

(young waitress) was to be eye candy, to be fondled if the opportunity arose and not have an opinion on anything. I don't nor did I feel affronted by any of this. It was how it was in that era and even now the thing that irritates me the most about this was that my opinion didn't matter!

I spent two and a half years at The Stag and left to take a chef's job. When my first baby was born in 1986, like most young families, we were living on a shoestring. Michael was only a few weeks old when I got a call out of the blue from Michel asking if I would work on the Saturday night because he was short of staff. I remember the relief that I would be getting £10 for that shift. I worked most Saturday nights after that and some evenings. I worked there on a part time basis when the head chef was Patrick Vervoux with his wife Andrea. That was The Stag's nouvelle cuisine period.

In 1988, Simon Sparrow started work as head chef. It is no secret that by 1990 we were in love. Michel sacked me.

I guess I was more dispensable than the head chef.

Sometime in 2013, we went to look at The Stag with a view to taking on the tenancy. At the time Charles Wells had great plans to knock through the bar to open the pub up into one big dining space and they were looking for a couple to invest and take on the new look. I was adamant that the public bar had to stay intact for the village and thought knocking through was a ridiculous idea that would not be beneficial to the business. I laugh at myself now I see what a great job is being done of the most recent refurb! I still

think, at the time, it was the right decision so we turned it down. At the time we were running The Wheatsheaf in Bow Brickhill which was also a Charles Wells pub. Sometime in 2014 Peter Wells (MD of Charles Wells) was in our pub and mentioned to us that The Stag was still looking for tenants. I said we would love to take it on but didn't want to take it in the direction the brewery did. His reply was that he was sure they could work something out. In October 2014, after a small refurb, Simon and I took over the tenancy at The Stag.

I've never been any good at recognising famous people, but Stirling Moss was a regular visitor to The Stag in Michel's time and Brian Ferry had lunch there while he was shooting the video for Avalon at The Towers.

Michel was godfather to my eldest son Michael. We had a lovely relationship (even after he sacked me) and I always said that if I didn't already have such an amazing Dad, then Michel would have been my father figure.

Menus: when I was first there, quiche was on the menu as a starter. Also ravioli, which came out of a tin... I jest you not! Other starters were langoustine in garlic butter, globe artichoke with hollandaise sauce, fresh asparagus, moules and pâté.

Main courses were Michel's famous half roast duck, Dover sole, lobster thermidor, fillet rossini, steak diane, chicken Kiev which we had to present to the guest and then, with a sharp knife cut into it to expose the garlic butter oozing out.

The sweet trolley was laden with meringue Chantilly, sherry trifle, oranges in grand mariner, brandy snaps, chocolate & coffee pudding, green figs, fresh pineapple with Kirsch, rum baba and fresh strawberries. At dessert we would wheel the trolley to each table, lifting it up and down the steps where necessary and guests could choose as much as they like...and often did!

Christmas was even busier than normal and for the fortnight before we had no days off because we would also be open on the Monday. Christmas day was a very long lunch shift with customers leaving at 6pm-ish and afterwards Michel would get Christmas dinner for all of us to eat together. It was the only time we ever saw Helen, his wife.

Sometimes (not often) Michel would do an outside function. We did some of these at The Towers when the Yogis were there. The Gold Room was the function room. It was stunning in every way, but downstairs where we had to prep and cook, there was nothing, literally just cold water available. Everything else had to be hired in.

LIZ ROBINSON

My great grandad lived 'next door but one' to The Stag and so it was definitely his local.

I worked there in 2006 or 2007 at a guess, so much further down the line. But my great grandad and his sons would have been in there all the time. We're talking about the Rickard family, who lived next door all their lives.

This is my great grandad and 7 of his daughters. My grandad's sisters. Grandad was one of 11.

George Rickard on the village Green with a daughter in law and his 7 surviving daughters (Doreen, the youngest daughter died as a young girl).

From left to right: wife of the oldest son, Albert, Kath Rickard, Win Saunders, Dorothy Thomas, George, Eva Aslett, Elsie Bonham.

Kneeling, Phyllis Rickard, Margaret Gibbs, Lily Howarth.

CHRIS SANSOME

I lived in Ledburn for 25 years at Ledburn Farm, I spent many hours in The Stag. I met my wife at The Stag. She is from New Zealand and we moved here over 20 years ago. My father owned a plane which was kept at nearby Ledburn and he took the photograph below of The Stag pub.

One of many visits to The Stag back in 2011.

ANGELA SOWTEN

My mother worked in the kitchen of The Stag under Michel for a good few years, and once I was old enough I had a Saturday job as washer-up and general dogsbody, so it's a place that's close to my heart.

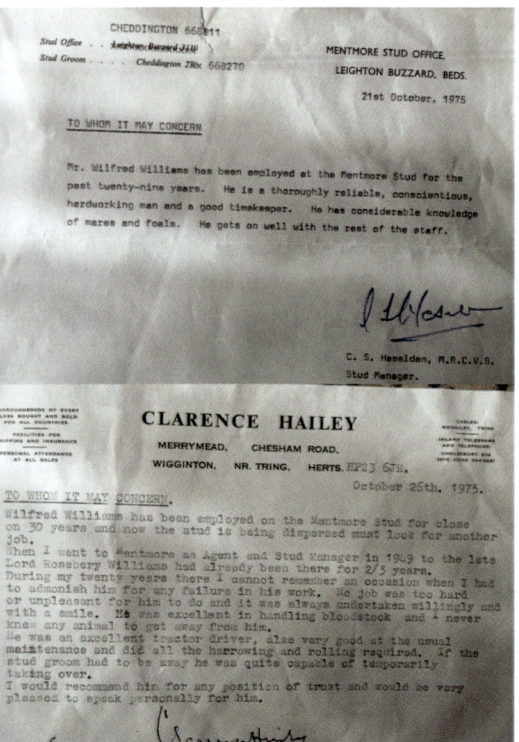

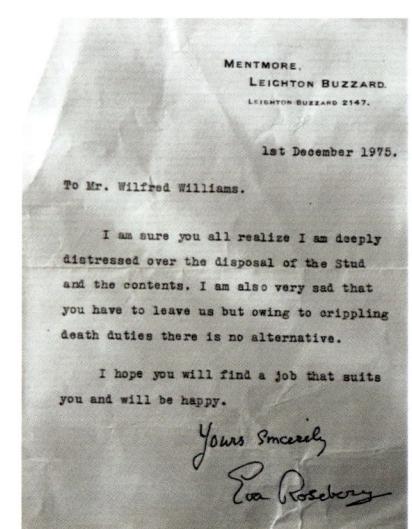

Letter and job reference belonging to Wilfred Williams (Angela Sowten's father).

Wilfred Williams and Fred Humphr

KAREN AND STEVE THOMAS

Our lasting first impression of The Stag, shortly after we moved to Mentmore in the late 1980s, was sitting in the public bar and seeing a huge bowl of *moules marinière* coming over the bar. This wasn't exactly burger-and-chips bar food! It was of course in Michel Rigal's time in charge; we count ourselves truly fortunate to have experienced not only Michel's cuisine, but also his care for the local community. No-one else has balanced the need to bring in diners from far and wide, with the need to maintain a local pub atmosphere as well as Michel did.

A good example comes from another early memory, of public bar regular George Pennell (occupant of Stone Lodge and then still doing gardening jobs at The Towers) sitting in the same corner seat with Graf, his "bad-tempered dog who didn't like strangers". We evidently weren't strangers, even at our first meeting, as Graf, a large Alsatian, would happily take his custard cream biscuits with no evidence of bad temper at all... we may just have wondered how Graf would have introduced George, were he capable of speech!

All three of our children have worked at The Stag, which helped me achieve a lifetime's ambition of having each of my offspring pull me a pint – though the youngest, Sally, had to be called from her real job in the kitchen specially for the purpose!

It has been desolate to see the fire in the village go out on the recent occasions The Stag has been forced to close for extended periods. It's been a privilege to be able to contribute in a small way as shareholders now it is owned and run by and for the village. We hope it will be the home of happy future memories for us and for many others.

The Stag at night by Steve Thomas.

JULIE THOMSON

Under Denise and Simon we saw The Stag transform into a high-end restaurant with the best service and incredible food. Our daughter Amelia, now eight, adored the food and was always made extremely welcome.

The Stag became a place we'd go to for special occasions with family, for Sunday roasts, and for drinks and nibbles in the garden. The fish was exceptional and the Mediterranean king prawns were finger-licking delights, even for a three year old!

We have fond memories of the garden which was kept beautifully, the huge fig tree, and the lovely piano that was often played. Visits to The Stag felt special and whilst you were there, nothing else mattered. This was largely down to the brilliant, friendly service that was focussed on excellence and the fact each course served took your taste buds on a delectable journey.

RITA TOMKINS

My mum used to go to The Stag to pay our rent, to what they called the Estate Office. The name Mr Dix comes to mind, but I could be wrong, that would have been pre 1960. I know mum went to The Stag at Mentmore, she definitely did not go to Ledburn to pay her rent, but that was pre-1960, so in 1969 they may have gone to the Manor House, but we had moved away then.

My dad worked in the gardens and we lived in Crafton, most of the cottages were owned by Merchant Adventurer properties and some were owned by Rosebery, who always kept them in good repair.

The Merchant Venturer's bought a lot of cottages and land off the Rosebery family in 1944.

CLAIRE WARREN

My experience of The Stag was in the 1970s. My mother was friendly with Michel and I had my first Saturday job there washing up.

Michel was a great friend of the family, and we regularly used to eat there for many a big family occasion, including my 21st birthday when my sister drank too much and was sick on the front door step.

Michel used to do a fabulous escargot in garlic butter. I can remember eating it when I was only 15 years old. It was a sad day when he gave up The Stag, and moved to the Kennels at Ascot until he died.

IRENE AND JOHN WEBSTER

We lived in Aldbury, but belonged to Mentmore Golf Club and regularly would go to The Stag for a drink or lunch after playing golf.

After a country walk, we would sit by the fire and read the newspapers and enjoy some of the local characters' conversations which we indulged in. The proprietor, being a larger than life character himself was very welcoming and lively.

We would often bring friends to the pub who were visiting from various parts of the world and we would enjoy an excellent meal. To this day, these visitors recall the happy times they had.

We remember the children's garden with rabbits and chickens too.

A few years later we moved to Mentmore and continued to frequent the bar and restaurant. The garden was so enjoyable in the summer, such a nice place to be and we could walk home!

Having a tour of the pub whilst being refurbished, it was fascinating to think that the cellar was much the same as the beginning of the pub. I just had to hold the original chain that held the barrels in place. Nostalgic I know, but so much part of the pub's history.

We are really happy The Stag is going to reopen and once again be the hub of the village. So three cheers for all the hard work taking place refurbishing the pub.

RUTH WHEELER

I was born in 1934. My mother was the eldest of twelve children. Her parents Ruth and George Rickard lived in an estate house in Mentmore, my grandfather George was a bricklayer working for the then Lord Rosebery.

My first memory of The Stag, as a very small child, was the landlord – Jack Nash driving his taxi. Very few people had cars then and his taxi was the only vehicle in the village. There was a bus that ran on Tuesdays (market day) and on Sundays to Leighton Buzzard. If villagers needed transport it was Jack they called. I believe he was quite busy, although the younger people cycled.

Local men supported The Stag, my grandfather was one of the best customers! Lord Rosebery ran two horse studs one in Mentmore and one in adjoining Crafton.

He employed a number of grooms most of whom enjoyed a drink in The Stag of an evening. I believe Mr. Nash did a good trade. His wife was involved in the running of the pub but it was a lady by the name of Mrs Wioland who was seen the most. I may be wrong but I think she was Mrs Nash's sister. Mrs Wioland had a daughter - Alwyn and a son Gerald.

My parents moved to Linslade, but I still spent a lot of time in Mentmore. For years The Stag was a typical village pub, sawdust on the floor and a tap room – I never knew what that meant!

The gent's toilet block to the left of the pub was demolished years ago. In recent years it became very upmarket relying on trade from outside the village.

There is a very nice picture of The Stag taken many years ago with a few locals standing around. I have the picture hanging on my sitting room wall and there was one just inside the pub.

ALAN WIRTH

My great grandfather, James Smith, was the head gardener at Mentmore for some years around 1900. My grandfather met and married one of his daughters and both kept personal diaries of the time they were at Mentmore. I have both of those diaries and they record their many bicycle and trap trips to Leighton Buzzard and local villages.

The postcard below was sent by my great aunt Ada Smith who previously lived in the Manor House at Mentmore, to my grandfather Sydney Smith in 1923. She mentions "Joe" who I think is Joe Roads, a prominent landowner from the area.

Sydney Wallace Smith was my grandfather who had returned to Australia with my grandmother and my mother and two other children. Ada, her sister, married Joe Roads.

My great grandfather and great grandmother are buried in the graveyard along with their son who was only a child. His grave is quite special because Lady Rothschild paid for it.

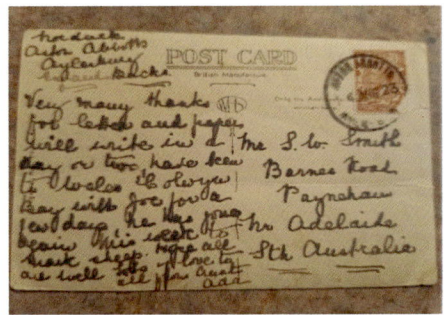

This photo is of the wedding of my grandmother and grandfather in front of the head gardener's house.

CAROLINE YEO

The Stag was where I met my future husband Adrian, so I have many fond memories of both the pub and the village.

Adrian was one of the few people who could play the old out-of-tune piano in the public bar, and often accompanied the scratch 'jazz' band with Rodney on tea chest bass, and someone else on the washboard.

There was also the vociferous opposition to the 'modernisation' of the public bar, replacing the practical linoleum with carpet! This meant that we all had to wipe our boots and wellies on the way in.

When I worked as a barmaid with the redoubtable Janet Inglis, I broke a glass in the sink while washing up. The crack was distinctly heard and, after a few seconds of silence, those in the bar let out a loud cheer.

FUN, FOOD AND FROLICS

Community events have been taking place in Mentmore for centuries and still do to this day from auctions to arts festivals, from retirement parties to Le Mans send-offs.

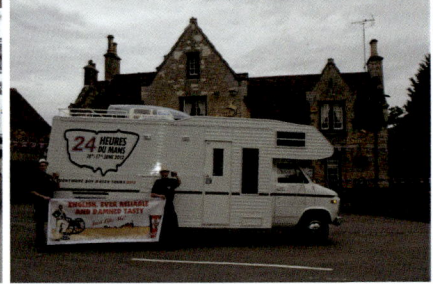

Activities in the pub and on The Green, which the community all participate in one way or another, include summer fetes, VE Day celebrations, quizzes, plant sales, barn dances, art festivals, live music events, charity events and BBQ's. Many months of planning behind the scenes goes into every event to make it the success it always is.

Ex-resident Howard Wells arranged a series of dinners on a regular basis which included after-dinner speakers. One such speaker was Dame Mary Peters who became the most successful athlete in Northern Irish history.

Musical interludes with Wild Willy Barrett were a popular evening in the public bar. There was an old upright piano, a tea-chest, bass drum and a washboard, all in regular use. Rodney, another ex-resident, would often play either the tea-chest or the washboard.

The Mentmore people continue to raise money for many charities and they certainly deserve a medal for all their hard work and dedication.

More fun and games, from tug of war to penny for the guy and vegetable contests.

Former Formula One racing driver Mark Webber and his wife Ann Neal owned and ran the pub for several years. Mark regularly organised cycle events such as "Ride the Horns" below in 2008, with the finish line being at The Stag.

COMMUNITY BUY THE STAG

Shock, horror the pub closed!!!

With disbelief the community read the newsletter stating the pub was closed with immediate effect.

Many people were very sad when they had heard the pub had closed. Some had bookings for celebrations which had to be cancelled virtually overnight.

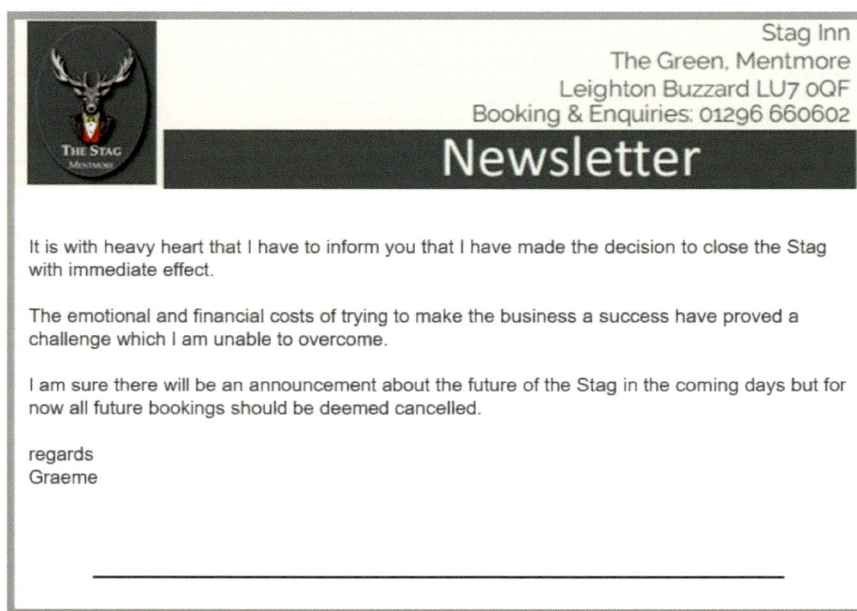

Stag Inn
The Green, Mentmore
Leighton Buzzard LU7 0QF
Booking & Enquiries: 01296 660602

Newsletter

It is with heavy heart that I have to inform you that I have made the decision to close the Stag with immediate effect.

The emotional and financial costs of trying to make the business a success have proved a challenge which I am unable to overcome.

I am sure there will be an announcement about the future of the Stag in the coming days but for now all future bookings should be deemed cancelled.

regards
Graeme

The pub was then up for sale. Owner Charles Wells Brewery kindly allowed the following sales brochure photos to be included here. The pub was on the market in 2018.

HOW 42 PEOPLE ENDED UP BUYING THEIR LOCAL PUB!
BY PETER BRAZIER

In October 2018, suddenly and without notice, the pub was empty again. The last tenancy had been unusual to say the least. I had just personally experienced the process of the loss of a nearby local pub, the Carpenters Arms in Slapton. I attended the planning committee meeting, which needed little persuasion to allow change of use to residential. It was too easy to demonstrate how it was not a viable going concern. The Parish Council had tried previously the get The Stag registered as a Community Asset but the legal team at the then District Council would not have it, not a good sign and I was preparing for a battle. Shortly after The Stag had closed, I bumped into Adam Goran and we were standing outside the pub and somehow the discussion got onto how we could possibly run it as a community. After thinking about it for a day or two I plucked up the courage to phone the brewery and found the right person to speak to. It wasn't a very straightforward conversation because the brewery did not have an operating model for a community run pub. Their only vision for The Stag was of a couple, living in, one front of house one in the kitchen, with the offering being only a high-end restaurant.

We always saw the potential for a café there, with trade provided by the passing daytime traffic, I didn't get it. Nevertheless, I asked them for their business plan template and when Adam and I looked at the onerous operating conditions and overheads, we decided it would be impossible to take it on and left it there.

Back with my Parish Council hat on, I was expecting the planning application for change of use to residential to come through but after a few months we heard through the grapevine that the freehold was up for sale. After checking in with Adam that he had the energy to go at it again, I got on the phone and I eventually found out which agent was handling the sale. I made a call and expressed an interest. When I discovered that their asking price was around half a million I realised it was a do-able project and so Adam and I got together, brought Bob Ager on board and we started to look seriously at how we would go about rallying the community together to raise the funds to buy the pub. On the 12th July 2019 we formally made an offer to the brewery to purchase the freehold of The Stag including all its contents for £475,000. We were fully expecting them to push us up.

We then drafted some documents with a vision for how the pub would look and feel under community ownership. We then produced a small leaflet which we hand delivered to everyone in Mentmore, Crafton, Ledburn, Rowden Farm and anywhere else we could reach. The leaflet invited everybody to a meeting in the Village Hall on the 22nd July 2019 at 7:30pm. We set out about 20 chairs and we had a short presentation ready. We really did not know what to expect but as people showed up we had to empty the store of chairs with over 60 people inside the Hall and a further 30, who were outside literally hanging in through the windows. I had prepared a script about preparing our vision statement, but I didn't get beyond the first sentence. I said that the reason we are here tonight is to save The Stag, I was stopped by a round of applause and I had to let Adam and Bob do the rest. The support we got from everyone was overwhelming. The game was on!

We realised the three of us knew little about running a hospitality business nor had the right financial experience, so we recruited Caroline Gates and Nick Walters and formed the board of directors of "The Stag at Mentmore Ltd."

We spent the next couple of months personally visiting everybody who expressed an interest to explain how we were going to do this, the tax incentives and how the shareholder structure would work. In the background however, we were getting no word from the agent as to whether or not the brewery was prepared to accept our offer and in September we were told that they were considering another offer for the pub. We were told that it was an operator and not a developer and so we were reassured by that. The whole reason we set this up was to save The Stag and if saving it meant letting someone else buy it for the right reasons that was fine.

So we took the foot off the gas of collecting shareholder pledges, while waiting to hear from the agent. We chased on a regular basis and we thought it was lost until on the 8th November 2019, a phone call to the agent revealed the fact that the other party had pulled out and it was now obvious that we were the only offer left. By the end of the month, they had accepted our offer and the long and slow process of drawing up, exchanging and completing started. We had to revisit the pledges and get surveys done on the building. We lost a lot of time over Christmas, but by January 2020 we had had a good survey result and set up contracts with our solicitors and tax advisors. We were ready to go. I went to our solicitors on the 24th January 2020 and signed the Head of Terms Agreement. Now that was an interesting moment, we had precisely £10 in the bank. However, in the end we can be extremely grateful to every last one of the 42 investors, because everybody who said they would put money in, did put the money in, on time, without fuss.

We formally exchanged contracts on 2nd March 2020 and completed on 6th March 2020.

The plan we had was just to decorate the pub, do some basic maintenance, get it ready and open in a couple of months. Of course, Covid changed all that. Before we even had a chance to get the paint brushes out, the famous "you must stay at home" announcement came from Boris Johnson on 23rd March 2020 and we didn't know which way to turn.

This photo was taken by myself and was featured in the Leighton Buzzard Observer who were also in attendance.

As it turned out the lockdown worked in our favour. We were well funded and had developed a vision to create a better place, so we were able to dig deeper into the renovation than we had ever expected to be able to do. We used the time to overhaul the building. We gave ourselves time to engage an architect to make the building and garden accessible, incorporating a disabled toilet and ramps to the garden to provide step free access. We opened up the building to make The Stag the pub we had envisioned. We even created a cycle hub to attract important daytime business. We were able to lift four layers of floors. When a pub is on a short-term tenancy agreement, they will do the minimum necessary to renovate and maintain so we needed to remove all that. By late summer it appeared the virus was under some level of control and so we set a target of opening in time for Christmas 2020. However, just as we were setting that out, we saw what was coming (further restrictions) and retreated, thankfully. It would have been a disaster to open and then shut a few weeks later. So, we had time to refine our plans and get more details right.

At the beginning of May 2021, we employed a general manager and head chef and aimed to open on 21st June 2021, hopefully with only a few Covid-related restrictions. Predicting the future, short or long term during those times turned out to be foolish. An interesting side story to this tale is that after the purchase, we received a pack of documents relating to the pub and in that pack was a copy of an email from the brewery to their solicitors instructing them to seek permission for change of use to residential, this was in 2014 just before Simon and Denise took over the pub.

The vision of owning and refurbishing the pub continued throughout lockdown in 2020 and 2021. It became a reality and thankfully the community help was overwhelming.

A building is just a building, but its warmth of village people over the years brings it to life and a new adventure.

There will no longer be "last orders" as The Stag continues its journey.

> • Sometime during the tenure of Thomas Hicks, but probably in the mid-1920s, the king-stone in the arch of the porch at The Stag was dropping, so the estate builders (Albert Rickard, Len Humphrey and Albert's dad) were brought in to make the necessary repairs. The stone was acquired from Yirrells and was cut using a stone saw. Before completing the work, they placed a half-crown, a shilling and a sixpence inside an old lemonade bottle and buried it in the porch. Of course, this cannot be confirmed until such time as the porch needs another major rebuild!

The roof over the porch was leaking, and was the only serious source of damp in the building, so it was completely redone – it was rotten underneath, and this pile of 170 year old, hand made roofing nails were found there.

Crumpled newspaper from 27th January 1936. It was found in the wall and used to fill in the holes.

Giveaways (with donations to charities) from clearing out the pub.

The Rosebery Coat of Arms (a lion holding a primrose with an Earl's coronet) was carved on the front porch, however, over the years this as deteriorated and has been re-carved. Traditionally, most of the houses in the village had H & R (Hannah de Rosebery) carved in their stonework.

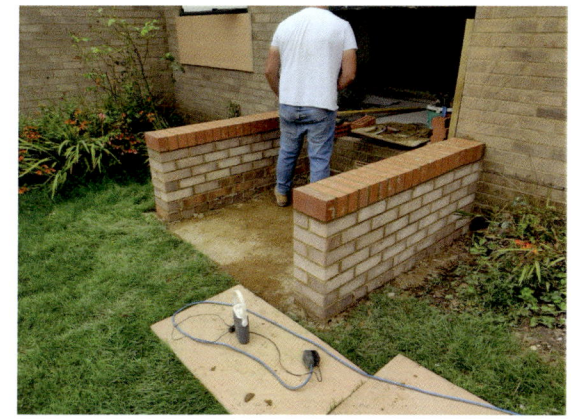

We've partnered with a local, award winning brewer to produce our own house ale. We're calling it 1847 as a nod to the year when The Stag first opened.

Greg Smith MP, April 2021

"It was wonderful to see progress on the renovations of The Stag in Mentmore over the summer. Local pubs are the beating heart of village communities and those bringing this much loved local back to life are community heroes.

It is sad that the Covid restrictions mean it cannot yet open, but it will be a truly wonderful day when The Stag re-opens its doors and we can all celebrate its renewal and the end to Covid restrictions."

EDDY - HEAD CHEF

Eddy McLean Hall joined the pub on 1st May 2021 as head chef. Eddy began his career at The Stag in 2011 as a waiter and commis chef. Over the years, he has worked at many farms, butchers, pubs and restaurants and most recently was head chef at Nonna's in Woburn Sands.

His first Saturday was fully booked, which he was very excited about, as were we all.

His flair for food is traditional with a twist, using locally sourced, seasonal products. He has already started growing vegetables in the kitchen garden at The Stag.

ALESSIO - FRONT OF HOUSE LEAD

Alessio Melis began his hospitality career at "Da Nico", a family run traditional restaurant in a small town in North Sardinia, where he learned the trade whilst studying to complete his hospitality diploma.

Since then he has worked in many prestigious establishments, both in Sardinia and England. He has won many awards in his career.

After relocating to Mentmore in late 2019, Alessio joined The Stag as front of house lead just after the pub opened.

Present directors of The Stag:

Robert Ager

Peter Brazier

Caroline Gates

Adam Goran

Nicholas Walters

In total, there are 42 shareholders.

The Stag opened its doors to the public on Monday 21st June 2021.

19th century roots, 21st century experience.

It's been quite the journey!

In 2018, on the sudden departure of the previous tenants, The Stag was once again closed. Charles Wells struggled to find replacement tenants and put it up for sale. The local community was horrified at the thought of losing their beloved pub and even more fearful that it might be sold for residential development. Therefore, a small group of locals decided that rather than risk this possibility they would see if it was viable to purchase the pub as a community asset.

After protracted negotiations with the brewery, a price was agreed and following a village meeting, enough money was raised to fund the purchase, pay for a complete refurbishment and provide enough working capital to re-open and run the pub. Today The Stag is owned by 42 local shareholders who are united in their desire to provide a great drinking and eating experience for locals and visitors alike.

The pub you see today has been completely refurbished and the gardens have been relandscaped. We are enormously proud of this accomplishment and would like to thank the many contractors who have made this possible. We hope you like what you see and that you enjoy your time with us.

To the never ending journey of The Stag ... CHEERS!

CONTRIBUTORS

My heartfelt thanks to all those who have contributed to this book. Your community driven enthusiasm, trips down memory lane, photos and stories have made this book what it is. I thank you all!

Robert Adams	Robert Gates	Kate and Ken Payne
Bob Ager	Heather Gill	Terry Payne
Jenny Allen	Netta Glover	Ian Perry
Diane and Mike Armson	Daisy Goyen	Richard Phillips
Carol Armstrong	Corinne Griffin	Sarah Randall
Mike Buckle	Deborah Hale-Hall	Denise Redding
Bucks History Society	Andrea Hanson	Sami Rich
Bucks Herald Newspaper	Fiona Harrison	Liz Robinson
Peter Brazier	James Henderson	Rev. Howard Robson
Angie and Stan Bowles	Pete Humphrey	Chris Sansome
Michael Buckle	David Hutton-Potts	Greg Smith MP
Mary Casserley (marycasserley.com)	Rosie Knight	Angela Sowten
Charles Wells Brewery	The Langley Family	Simon Sparrow
Malcolm Cleland	Stella Marshall	Karen Thomas
Andrew Cooke	Eddy McLean Hall	Steve Thomas
Carol and Terry Cox	Alessio Melis	Julie Thomson
Liz and Nigel Dack	Mentmore Society Archive	Rita Tonkins
Philip Delafield	Robert Mildred	Claire Warren
Linda Draper	John and Jenny Morris	John and Irene Webster
Craig Eckloff	Nan Morrison	Ruth Wheeler
Dawn Forest	Rose Norton	Ashley Wiggins
Darrel Foster-Kirsop	Paul O'Carroll	Alan Wirth
Caroline and Martin Gates	Diane Payne	Caroline Yeo

WHEN A STORY BECOMES A MEMORY, THE MEMORY BECOMES A TREASURE.

Stories to be told,

By the people with hearts of gold.

With wildlife in abundance,

All seen at a glance.

They all know there is so much more,

To our little village named "Mentmore".

A village with its famously historic towers,

Set in the countryside surrounded by wild flowers.

Not forgetting the amazing fetes,

Run with military precision, BBQs, teas and homemade cakes.

The volunteers with their eager hands,

Prepare with gusto to set up their stands.

At Christmas time the tree goes up on The Green.

Carol singing, mince pies, mulled wine and the fairy lights gleam.

At every chance the community pulls together,

No matter the event, the season or the weather.

The Stag pub is open again and welcomes everyone.

Hooray! At last, another era has finally and thankfully come.

So "Cheers" to one and all. Here's to having less pandemics,

With plentiful drinks, food, fun and frolics.

Mentmore is a little treasure,

Stories from the Hart will live on forever.

IMAGE CREDITS